THE FUTURE OF FOREIGN INTELLIGENCE

OTHER BOOKS IN THE SERIES

Not a Suicide Pact
The Constitution in a Time of National Emergency
Richard A. Posner

Supreme Neglect
How to Revive Constitutional Protection for Private Property
Richard A. Epstein

Out of Range
Why the Constitution Can't End the Battle over Guns
Mark V. Tushnet

Unfinished Business
Racial Equality in American History
Michael J. Klarman

Is There a Right to Remain Silent?
Coercive Interrogation and the Fifth Amendment After 9/11
Alan M. Dershowitz

The Invisible Constitution
Laurence H. Tribe

Uninhibited, Robust, and Wide-Open
A Free Press for a New Century
Lee C. Bollinger

From Disgust to Humanity
Sexual Orientation and Constitutional Law
Martha C. Nussbaum

The Living Constitution
David A. Strauss

Keeping Faith with the Constitution
Goodwin Liu, Pamela S. Karlan, Christopher H. Schroeder

Cosmic Constitutional Theory
Why Americans Are Losing Their Inalienable Right to Self-Governance
J. Harvie Wilkinson III

More Essential Than Ever
The Fourth Amendment in the Twenty First Century
Stephen J. Schulhofer

On Constitutional Disobedience
Louis Michael Seidman

The Twilight of Human Rights Law
Eric A. Posner

Constitutional Personae
Cass R. Sunstein

The Future of Foreign Intelligence
Privacy and Surveillance in a Digital Age
Laura K. Donohue

INALIENABLE RIGHTS SERIES

. . .

SERIES EDITOR
Geoffrey R. Stone

Geoffrey Stone and Oxford University Press gratefully acknowledge the interest and support of the following organizations in the Inalienable Rights series: The ALA; The Chicago Humanities Festival; The American Bar Association; The National Constitution Center; The National Archives

The Future of Foreign Intelligence

Privacy and Surveillance in a Digital Age

Laura K. Donohue

OXFORD
UNIVERSITY PRESS

OXFORD
UNIVERSITY PRESS

Oxford University Press is a department of the University of Oxford. It furthers the University's objective of excellence in research, scholarship, and education by publishing worldwide. Oxford is a registered trade mark of Oxford University Press in the UK and certain other countries.

Published in the United States of America by Oxford University Press
198 Madison Avenue, New York, NY 10016, United States of America.

Cataloging-in-Publication Data is on file with the Library of Congress
ISBN 978–0–19–023538–3

3 5 7 9 8 6 4 2
Printed by Sheridan, USA

Dedicated to

Peter S. Bing

and

Lily Donohue-Ozyar

Contents

. . .

Editor's Note

...

> We hold these truths to be self-evident, that all men are created equal, that they are endowed by their Creator with certain unalienable Rights....
>
> —*The Declaration of Independence*

The Fourth Amendment to the Constitution guarantees that "the right of the people to be secure in their persons, houses, papers, and effects, against unreasonable searches and seizures, shall not be violated." In the world of the Framers, the meaning of "search" was fairly clear. A "search" occurred when agents of the government entered an individual's home, or opened his mail, or rummaged through his suitcase in order to find something they were looking for. A "search," in other words, was a physical intrusion into a physical space owned or controlled by the person being "searched."

With the advent of new technologies, however, that definition of "search" came to be seen as too crabbed. Is a wiretap of a phone call a "search" even if the government agents do not physically enter to the target's home or office? Although the Supreme Court originally held that wiretapping is not a "search" for this reason, in

1967 the Court reversed itself and held that the Fourth Amendment "protects people, not places." In a world of changing technology, the critical issue, the Court held, is not whether government agents physically intruded into an individual's physical space, but whether they violated the individual's "reasonable expectations of privacy." That understanding, of course, created problems of its own. How do we define "reasonable expectations of privacy"?

Edward Snowden's revelation of a broad range of previously secret NSA surveillance programs brought this question to a head. In the years after the tragic events of September 11, 2001, government officials—including not only members of the intelligence community, but also presidents, judges, and members of Congress—approved dozens of new surveillance programs in an effort to keep our nation safe from further terrorist attacks. Faced with the threat of possible nuclear, chemical, biological, and conventional attacks on the homeland, and bearing the responsibility of preventing those attacks in a world in which "connecting the dots" was essential, the United States sought to strike an appropriate "balance" between the right of privacy and the national security.

But were the surveillance programs created in this environment of crisis consistent with the Fourth Amendment? Did these programs violate "reasonable expectations of privacy"? And if they constituted "searches" within the meaning of the Fourth Amendment, were they "reasonable"?

In *The Future of Foreign Intelligence*, Laura Donohue explores the origin and nature of the nation's post-9/11 surveillance programs, illuminates the fundamental meaning of the Fourth Amendment, examines the extent to which these new foreign intelligence programs can be reconciled with the core values of our Constitution, and highlights the danger that when we dilute our expectations of privacy in the context of foreign intelligence we risk undermining our legal and constitutional protection of privacy in more general criminal investigations as well.

By identifying and carefully analyzing these issues, Laura Donohue offers critical new insights that will help guide us as we explore the future of foreign intelligence.

—Geoffrey R. Stone
February 2016

The United States Foreign Intelligence Surveillance Court has appointed Professor Laura Donohue to serve as an amicus curiae. She wrote this book before the United States government granted her access to any classified information. Because of this, the government did not review her book for classified information.

Acknowledgments

Special thanks to Betsy Kuhn, David McBride, Geoffrey Stone, and Craig Timberland for reading the manuscript and offering valuable suggestions during the editing process. Their comments proved central to clarifying my thoughts, as well as the text, and were much appreciated.

The writing similarly benefited from the insights offered by a number of my colleagues. Randy Barnett, Kathy Chen, Dan Ernst, Erin Kidwell, John Mikhail, Jim Oldham, Julie O'Sullivan, Brad Snyder, David Super, Bill Treanor, and Peter Winn provided thoughtful critique. Ladislas Orsy kindly helped to verify the meaning of the Latin sources. Discussions with Bill Banks, John Bates, William Cuddihy, Mary DeRosa, Jameel Jaffer, Orin Kerr, David Kris, Robert Litt, David Medine, Marc Rotenberg, Julian Sanchez, Nadine Strossen, Bob Turner, and Sheldon Whitehouse provided deeper insight into many of the questions associated with the collection of foreign intelligence. Participants in the Georgetown Law Faculty Workshop, as well as the Privacy Law Scholars Conference contributed through dialogue. The students in Randy Barnett's

Constitutional Law Seminar read an early draft and raised important questions. Christine Ciambella, Ellen Noble, Thanh Nguyen, and Morgan Stoddard assisted tremendously in obtaining research materials.

As with any book, the ideas developed over time. I worked through the arguments in a series of law review articles from which the text of the final manuscript draws. The articles include *The Original Fourth Amendment*, 83 UNIV. OF CHICAGO L. REV. (2016); *The Dawn of Social Intelligence (SOCINT)*, DRAKE L. REV. (2015); *Section 702 and the Collection of International Telephone and Internet Content*, 38(1) HARV. J. OF L. & PUB. POL'Y (2015); *High Technology, Consumer Privacy, and U.S. National Security*, Symposium on *Corporate Counterterrorism*, 4(1) BUSINESS L. REV. (2015); *Bulk Metadata Collection: Statutory and Constitutional Considerations*, 37(3) HARV. J. OF L. & PUB. POL'Y, 757–900 (2014); and *FISA Reform*, 10(2) I/S: A J. OF L. & POL'Y FOR THE INFO. SOCIETY (2014). The editorial teams on each of these journals provided helpful feedback.

Numerous opportunities to present my research and to engage in public debate contributed to the final book. In particular, I would like to extend my thanks to the American Bar Association (ABA) Standing Committee on Law and National Security; the ABA Criminal Justice Section; the ABA Administrative Law Section; the American University Washington School of Law; the Cato Institute; the Electronic Privacy Information Center; the Federalist Society; the History Department at the University of Colorado, Boulder; the German Historical Institute; Marshall University; the Rotary Club of Leesburg, Virginia; the U.S. Senate Committee on the Judiciary; Westminster College; the University of Minnesota Law School; the University of Virginia School of Law; and Yale Law School.

Throughout my research, Dr. Peter Bing has been steadfast in his support, advice, and friendship. In an expression of my gratitude,

I dedicate this book to him, and to Lily. I deeply appreciate the support of my family, particularly my husband, Tansel, and my daughters Jasmine, Ayla Rose, and Lily, who are a constant source of inquiry and delight.

—Laura K. Donohue
Washington, DC

THE FUTURE OF FOREIGN INTELLIGENCE

Introduction

SINCE THE EARLY days of the Republic, political and military leaders have recognized that U.S. national security depends upon the collection of intelligence. On June 13, 1777, the New Hampshire Committee of Safety tipped off the Provincial Congress in Massachusetts that the British were planning to send troops to occupy the hills surrounding Boston. The army immediately used the information to its advantage. Colonel William Prescott led 1,200 soldiers to build defenses on the contested ground and caught the British flat-footed. British troops ultimately prevailed, but they suffered heavy losses, with more than one thousand men wounded or killed. The Battle of Bunker Hill ignited colonial morale and sent a message across the Atlantic that the war would not be won either quickly or easily.

During the Revolution, intelligence continued to play a key role. George Washington spent more than 10 percent of his military funds on surveillance. He established networks of agents throughout the northeast to collect information and report back to him.

As Washington explained to Elias Dayton, who directed the operation on Staten Island, "the necessity of procuring good Intelligence, is apparent."[1]

Peace brought with it new demands—not least for information to help the president negotiate the perilous waters of diplomacy. In his first State of the Union address, Washington requested a "competent fund" to finance foreign affairs. Within six months Congress established the Contingent Fund of Foreign Intercourse, known as the "secret service fund," to be used by Washington, as Senator John Forsyth explained, "for spies, if the gentleman so pleases." John Adams, Thomas Jefferson, James Madison, and subsequent presidents all went on to acknowledge the need for insight into foreign countries.

Absent information about threats, the country is in peril. Accordingly, Congress and the courts have given the executive latitude in how it obtains intelligence from abroad. Congress has overlaid deference with institutional design. Agencies focused on matters outside the country have been given greater leeway and allowed to operate in a more secretive environment than would ordinarily be countenanced. The 1947 National Security Act, for example, prohibits the director of the Central Intelligence Agency from having any domestic "police, subpoena, law-enforcement powers or internal-security functions." Instead, the agency's primary focus is the collection of human intelligence overseas.

To protect the rights of American citizens, more restrictions have accompanied surveillance conducted inside the United States. Starting in 1978, this meant that domestic electronic surveillance undertaken for national security purposes had to comport with the Foreign Intelligence Surveillance Act. The statute provided heightened protections for U.S. citizens. It created a special court to oversee the process, and it required congressional oversight of the intelligence agencies.

The problem that we now face is that the law is no longer sufficient to guard our rights. The world is suddenly and radically changing. New means of collecting and analyzing citizens' information threaten individual liberty and risk upsetting the balance of power in the United States.

Four phenomena have played a crucial role in this transformation. First, new technologies have dramatically expanded the amount and type of information that can be obtained, stored, and analyzed. Advances in computer science have made more of our lives accessible to industry and to the government. Our interactions with others have multiplied and become digitized. Social media takes private relationships online where they can be observed and recorded. New algorithms can be applied to generate information that even we may not know about ourselves. Technology can be used to build a comprehensive view of formal and informal networks to which we belong, power relationships within and between groups, and levels of intimacy between us and others. Because this information is digitized, it can be combined with other data, shedding even more light on the private sphere. Geolocational information provided by remote biometric identification, RFID chips, or GPS devices generates further insight into where we go, what we do, and who we are with when we do so.

Second, even as technology has increased the information available, the government has expanded its authority to gain access to the data. New statutes, executive orders, and internal guidelines have relaxed restrictions previously in place. Over the past decade, legal interpretations, often crafted in secret, have authorized broad interpretations of the language involved.

Third, the geographic assumptions built into the law to protect citizens' privacy no longer hold. The advent of cloud computing and global communication networks means that data, correspondence, and conversations no longer stay within domestic bounds. Information flows freely across the Internet, as efficiency, not users, determines where it goes. Documents and communications that previously would have been given higher levels of protection are thus now subject to surveillance.

Fourth, since the events of 9/11 there has been a convergence between national security and domestic law enforcement. As a consequence, the changes that have occurred have not been limited to foreign intelligence. The government can use its national security authorities, which incorporate standards considerably weaker than those in criminal law, to prosecute ordinary crime. The shift undermines individual rights across the board.

The accumulation of power resulting from these changes risks enormous political and social harm, as well as the potential for the executive branch to override the structural constraints under which it historically has been placed. The stakes could not be higher as we confront the digital age. To understand the profound change that has occurred, it is helpful to take account of the contours of the law prior to September 11, 2001.

HISTORY OF ABUSE

In 1971, a small group of anti-war activists calling themselves the Citizens' Commission to Investigate the Federal Bureau of Investigation (FBI) broke into a two-person FBI office in Pennsylvania. Timing the break-in for the night of the Muhammad Ali-Joe Frazier fight, they stole one thousand classified documents, which they then sent in batches to carefully chosen journalists and members of Congress. *WIN Magazine*, published by the War Resisters League, subsequently published all of the stolen documents. A code word on these papers, "COINTELPRO" (for "counterintelligence program"), prompted NBC reporter Carl Stern to initiate a Freedom of Information Act lawsuit. On December 6, 1973, he filed a story that ran on *NBC Nightly News*. "Secret FBI memos made public today show the late J. Edgar Hoover ordered a nationwide campaign to disrupt the activities of the New Left," explained newsman John Chancellor, who introduced the report. "He ordered his agents not only to expose New Left groups, but to take action against them to neutralize them."[2] The report detailed extensive domestic surveillance and disruption undertaken by the FBI targeting mostly left-wing groups and serving no law enforcement purpose.

Soon afterwards, Seymour Hersh, an investigative reporter for *The New York Times*, published an article that catapulted the conversation forward. He reported that during the Nixon administration the Central Intelligence Agency (CIA) had conducted a massive intelligence operation "against the antiwar movement and other dissident groups in the United States." A special unit had maintained intelligence files on more than 10,000 Americans, including members of Congress. The CIA had engaged in dozens of other illegal operations since the 1950s, including "break-ins, wiretapping, and the surreptitious inspection of mail."[3]

The allegations prompted both houses of Congress to create temporary committees to investigate: the House Select Committee on Intelligence, and the Senate Select Committee to Study Governmental Operations with Respect to Intelligence Activities. The latter, chaired by Idaho Democrat Senator Frank F. Church, was a carefully constructed, bipartisan initiative. The committee took testimony from hundreds of people, inside and outside of government, in public and private hearings.

The Church Committee found that domestic surveillance programs, conducted under the guise of foreign intelligence, had undermined the privacy rights of U.S. citizens. The National Security Agency (NSA) figured largely in its concerns.

The NSA, founded in secret in 1952 without a charter, was virtually unknown to most Americans at the time. "One has to search far and wide to find someone who has ever heard of the NSA," the Church Report noted, although the agency "employs thousands of people and operates with an enormous budget. Its expansive computer facilities comprise some of the most complex and sophisticated electronics machinery in the world."[4]

In the 1960s, the NSA began compiling a list of individuals subject to surveillance. The program, which operated from 1967 to 1973, started out by focusing on the international communications of Americans traveling to and from Cuba. It expanded to include individuals involved in civil disturbances, suspected of criminal activity, implicated in drug activity, of concern to those tasked with presidential protection, and suspected of involvement in international terrorism. In 1969 the program became known as Project MINARET. When Senators and members of the public learned of the program, they expressed alarm about its privacy implications. Central to critics' concerns was the potential for the collection programs to target communications of a wholly domestic nature.

Senator (later vice president) Walter Mondale articulated the Church Committee's disquiet: "Given another day and another President," he stated, "another perceived risk and someone breathing hot down the neck of the military leader then in charge of the NSA . . . my concern is whether that pressure could be resisted on the basis of the law or not." Mondale laid out the challenge: "[W]hat we have to deal with is whether this incredibly powerful and impressive institution . . . could be used by President 'A' in the future to spy upon the American people." To prevent this, Congress would have to be very careful to "define the law, spell it out so that it is clear what [the Director of the NSA's] authority is and . . . is not."[5]

During the Senate hearings into Project MINARET, committee members expressed concern about whether to make public a second, highly classified, large-scale surveillance program run by the NSA. The committee decided to discuss the program in open session on the grounds that it was illegal and contravened the Fourth Amendment.

Operation SHAMROCK was the cover name given to the program, in which the government had convinced three major telegraph companies to forward international telegraphic traffic to the Department of Defense. For nearly 30 years, the NSA and its predecessors received copies of most international telegrams that had originated in, or been forwarded through, the United States.

Initially, the program had focused on foreign targets. Like Project MINARET, though, the scope of the program had expanded. As new technologies became available, the NSA began extracting citizens' communications. It selected approximately 150,000 messages per month for analysis, distributing some of them to other agencies. Senator Frank Church recognized the problem created by new technologies: "In the case of the NSA, which is of particular concern to us today, the rapid development of technology in the area of electronic surveillance has seriously aggravated present ambiguities in the law." Church warned, "The broad sweep of communications interception by NSA takes us far beyond the previous Fourth Amendment controversies where particular individuals and specific telephone lines were the target."[6]

As the Senate hearings progressed, the House of Representatives took stock. The House Select Intelligence Committee, created in February 1975, was replaced five months later by a committee headed by Representative Otis Pike, a Democrat from New York. The Pike Committee similarly expressed concern about MINARET and SHAMROCK. The latter had resulted in the NSA maintaining files on 75,000 citizens between 1952 and 1974. These files included dossiers on civil rights leaders, antiwar activists, and even members of Congress. "For at least 13 years," the Committee found, "CIA employees were given unrestricted access to these files, and one or more worked full time retrieving information that presumably was contributed to the CIA's domestic intelligence program—Operation CHAOS—which existed from 1967 to 1974."[7] These programs violated statutory language and the Fourth Amendment.[8]

The Pike Committee expressed particular concern about the NSA's "vacuum cleaner" approach to foreign intelligence collection. In addition to international telephone calls, some 24 million telegrams and 50 million telex (teletype) messages entered, left, and transited the United States each year, and millions of additional messages traveled over leased lines—"including millions of computer data transmissions electronically entering and leaving the country."[9]

The NSA was not the only federal entity making use of new technologies to collect information on citizens. The FBI, CIA, Internal Revenue Service (IRS), U.S. Army, and others engaged in broad, domestic intelligence-gathering operations. These programs affected a staggering number of citizens. FBI headquarters maintained more than half a million domestic intelligence files. The CIA opened and photographed nearly a quarter of a million domestic first-class letters between 1953 and 1973, resulting in a computerized index of some one and a half million names. The FBI also opened hundreds of thousands of letters. Another 100,000 Americans were the subjects of Army intelligence files, even as the IRS maintained a database on 11,000 people based solely on political criteria.[10]

In each case, the initial purpose was to protect against national security threats. But the targets quickly expanded to include petty criminals and anyone with divergent political views.

REFORM

Coming on the heels of the Pentagon Papers, which demonstrated that the Johnson administration had systematically lied to the public and to Congress; the Watergate scandal, in which the Nixon administration orchestrated a break-in at the Democratic National Committee headquarters; and President Nixon's resignation, the news of the surveillance programs further eroded public confidence in the executive branch. Critical questions facing Congress were how to rebuild confidence in the federal government, how to incorporate new technologies into the existing infrastructure, and how to empower agencies to conduct electronic surveillance—all while protecting privacy.

A timely judicial decision helped to lay the groundwork. In 1967 the Supreme Court confronted new surveillance technologies—in this case, the placement of an electronic recording device on the outside of a telephone booth. In *Katz v. United States*, the Court replaced the Fourth Amendment doctrine that had required physical intrusion for a search to occur (and thus trigger the protections of the Fourth Amendment), with one centered on a reasonable expectation of privacy. The Court explained, "The fact that the electronic device employed to" record the target's conversation "did not happen to penetrate the wall of the phone booth can have no constitutional significance."[11] The Court left open the question of what procedures would be sufficient to satisfy the Fourth Amendment in the national security context.

Five years later, a case involving the bombing of a CIA office reached the courts. In *U.S. v. U.S. District Court*, the Supreme Court held that the electronic surveillance of domestic groups, even where security issues might be involved, required that the government first obtain a warrant. Justice Lewis Powell emphasized the limits of the decision: "[T]his case involves only the domestic aspects of national security. We have not addressed, and express no opinion as to, the issues which may be involved with respect to activities of foreign powers or their agents."[12] He suggested that the legislature might wish to consider new laws addressing foreign intelligence.

Congress took up the invitation and passed the 1978 Foreign Intelligence Surveillance Act (FISA). From the beginning, Congress made it clear that the law was designed to prevent the incursions into privacy represented by Project MINARET, Operation SHAMROCK, COINTELPRO, and other mass surveillance programs. With the passage of FISA, the Senate would "at long last place foreign intelligence electronic surveillance under the rule of law."[13]

FISA represented the culmination of a multibranch, multiyear, cross-party initiative directed at bringing the collection of foreign intelligence within a circumscribed legal framework. Congress consulted the NSA, FBI, CIA, and representatives of interested citizen groups, gaining broad support. The statute passed by significant majorities.

Congress inserted important protections to limit foreign intelligence collection inside the United States. Any information obtained from an electronic intercept had to be tied to a *specific* person or entity (identified as a foreign power or an agent of a foreign power), *before* any information could be collected. The phrase "foreign power" was a bit of a term of art: it meant a foreign government (or a group acting on behalf of, or controlled by, a foreign government); an entity engaged in international terrorism; or a foreign-based political organization substantially composed of noncitizens.

Another set of protections stemmed from concern evinced in the Senate about how to determine whether the target of the surveillance was a foreign power or an agent of a foreign power. The standard adopted was one of probable cause: the government must establish probable cause that a target is a foreign power or an agent of a foreign power *and* probable cause that the target is going to use the facilities to be placed under surveillance. This standard differed in important ways from that adopted in criminal law, where the government must establish probable cause that an individual is involved in criminal activity. In contrast, under FISA, foreigners can be placed under surveillance merely by acting on behalf, or at the behest, of a foreign government, whether or not it is recognized by the United States.

Foremost in legislators' minds was the need to provide heightened protections for U.S. citizens. Accordingly, for *citizens* to be considered an agent of a foreign power, they must knowingly engage in espionage or clandestine intelligence activities, undertake acts of sabotage or international terrorism (or aid, abet, or conspire to do the same), or enter the United States under a false identity. What this means is that, for citizens and permanent residents, the intelligence community must establish evidence of criminality *before* collection can begin. Collection, moreover, may not be initiated based on protected First Amendment activity.

Congress adopted procedures aimed at restricting the type of information that could be obtained and retained. As a further precaution against executive overreach, Congress provided for two new courts: the Foreign Intelligence Surveillance Court (FISC) and, to act in an appellate capacity, the Foreign Intelligence Surveillance Court of Review (FISCR). The purpose was to ensure that an independent, neutral, disinterested magistrate reviewed the strength of the government's case before it could place citizens under surveillance. Congress did not provide for opposing counsel. Instead, applications were made to the Court by the agency seeking the information. Where the government met the criteria and filed the appropriate forms, the judge's role was to enter an order as requested or to modify it accordingly.

During passage of FISA, to prevent a return to the abuses that had given rise to the need for legislation, Congress made it clear that the statute was to be the *only* way in which the president could conduct electronic surveillance inside the United States for foreign intelligence purposes. To underscore its position, Congress made it a felony, with up to five years' imprisonment, for anyone to conduct domestic electronic surveillance other than as provided for by statute.

Congress excluded three types of foreign intelligence collection from FISA: electronic communications *outside* U.S. borders, intelligence collection falling outside the statutory definition of "electronic communications," and the incidental collection of citizens' communications. The House Permanent Select Committee on Intelligence explained, "[T]he standards and procedures for overseas surveillance may have to be different than those provided in this bill for electronic surveillance within the United States."[14]

Executive Order 12333 subsequently set the guidelines for foreign intelligence collection (such as foreign-to-foreign electronic communications, intelligence collection outside of FISA's definition of "electronic communications," and the incidental collection of citizens' communications), as well as the other forms of surveillance. Issued by President Reagan in 1981, the order required each agency to establish procedures, approved by the attorney general, to govern such collection. The attorney general must "approve the use for intelligence purposes, within the United States or against a United States person abroad, of any technique for which a warrant would be required if undertaken for law enforcement purposes." Thus, surveillance could be undertaken only where the attorney general had "determined in each case that there [was] probable cause to believe that the technique is directed against a foreign power or an agent of a foreign power."

All electronic surveillance had to take place consistent with FISA *and* Executive Order 12333. The order directed the intelligence community to "use the least intrusive collection techniques feasible within the United States or directed against United States persons abroad."

TRADITIONAL FISA

Over the next two decades, Congress widened FISA's reach beyond governing the interception of electronic communications, creating what is collectively known as "traditional FISA."

The first expansion followed on the heels of the Aldrich Ames investigation. In 1985, Ames, who had worked for more than three decades for the CIA, turned coat and began supplying classified information to the Russian security services. Following Russia's capture and execution of undercover American agents, and observing Ames's sudden, unexplained wealth, the CIA opened a counterintelligence investigation. Agents searched his home and found documents that connected Ames to his Russian handlers. Upon his arrest, Ames confessed. It was not clear, however, that the search of his home had been legal.

Accordingly, in 1994 Congress amended FISA to include provision for physical search. The requirements are similar to those that mark electronic surveillance. To obtain an order from FISC, the government must first establish probable cause that the target of the search is a foreign power or an agent of a foreign power. The government may then examine premises, material, or property exclusively used or controlled by the target. As with electronic communications, heightened protections are afforded to citizens and to permanent residents.

In 1998, Congress again amended FISA, this time to allow for the installation and use of a pen register or trap-and-trace device.[15] A pen register is a device installed on a telephone that records the phone numbers of outgoing calls. A trap-and-trace device, on the other hand, acts as a caller ID, recording the numbers of all incoming calls. Under the law, the attorney general must submit an application in writing and under oath either to FISC or to a specially appointed magistrate to hear applications on behalf of the court. The document must include information demonstrating that the device has been, or will be, used by someone who is engaged in international terrorism, or is a foreign power or an agent of a foreign power. In the event of an emergency, the attorney general can authorize a so-called pen/trap order without judicial approval, as long as an application is submitted within a week.

In addition to physical search and pen/trap orders, Congress later amended FISA to allow for the collection of business records. The change stemmed from the 1995 Oklahoma City bombing, in which right-wing extremist Timothy McVeigh parked a Ryder rental truck packed with a fertilizer bomb outside the Murrah Federal Building. During the investigation, concern was raised about investigators' ability to obtain business records related to the truck rental, to a storage unit in Kansas, and to a locker in Arizona. Accordingly, in 1998, new statutory language gave the government the ability to obtain documents maintained by common carriers, public accommodation facilities, storage facilities, and vehicle rental facilities.

The breadth of the business records provision that was included in traditional FISA is of note. A common carrier is an individual or company that transports goods or passengers on regular routes at set rates. It includes buses, taxis, commercial airplanes, passenger trains, cruise ships, railroads, and trucking companies. Places of public accommodation encompass more than five million establishments, ranging from restaurants, hotels, theaters, convention centers, and shopping centers, to pharmacies, doctors' offices, museums, libraries, zoos, and schools.[16] As for storage facilities, by 2013, there were more than 48,500 in the United States, with about 10.85 million households renting a self-storage unit.[17] Car rental companies can now be found in more than 21,000 locations.[18]

To limit the reach of orders issued under the section, the records sought had to be for "an investigation to gather foreign intelligence information or an investigation concerning international terrorism." The application had to include "specific and articulable facts giving reason to believe that the person to whom the records pertain is a foreign power or an agent of a foreign power." Congress required agencies to follow the same steps as those taken with regard to electronic surveillance (submitting an application to FISC to obtain an order, which then compels the company to hand over the records).

Despite the government's request for broader authority, it made little use of its new powers. Between 1998 and 2001, the FBI submitted only one business records application to FISC.

In summary, by the turn of the 21st century, Congress had laid out a set of requirements that provided the executive branch with the flexibility to ascertain potential threats to U.S. national security from abroad, and to ensure stability within the United States. It simultaneously included provisions to protect citizens' privacy. For surveillance of U.S. citizens, in each of the four categories (electronic surveillance, physical search, pen/trap, and business records), some evidence of involvement in illegal activities had to be demonstrated *before* collection could begin. The targets were individualized, with particularized orders, issued by a court. The Senate and House intelligence committees provided oversight. To prevent the more flexible standards in national security from bleeding over into criminal law, the Department of Justice constructed a wall between foreign intelligence and law enforcement. Prosecutors and agents investigating matters related to ordinary crime could not use FISA. But intelligence agents could refer matters to law enforcement for prosecution of illegal activities linked to national security.

All of this was before the attacks on the World Trade Center and Pentagon.

In an instant, everything changed.

CHAPTER ONE

...

Imbalance

SEPTEMBER 11, 2001, upset an equilibrium that for decades had marked the collection of foreign intelligence. The Bush administration immediately assaulted the constraints under which the intelligence agencies had been required to operate. On September 19, 2001, Attorney General John Ashcroft presented a bill to Congress, demanding that legislators approve it within 48 hours. It was too early to know how the attack had been engineered; what, if anything, had gone amiss; and who was responsible for it. The 9/11 Commission Report, which did consider these questions, was not issued until July 26, 2004. But the attacks and the lives lost had shocked the country. Congress was poised to act. The intelligence community used the opportunity to roll back the restrictions carefully constructed in the 1970s. New technologies allowed for the massive collection of information and novel data mining methods offered the government powerful new tools.

Legislation sped through Congress under extraordinary procedures. The bill bypassed committee markup and went straight behind closed doors. Senator Patrick Leahy, chair of the Senate Judiciary Committee, and Representative Jim Sensenbrenner, chair of the House Judiciary Committee, along with other members of Congress, tried to work with the administration to redraft the bill. The House held only one hearing, in which Attorney General Ashcroft served as the sole witness. Unusually, neither the House nor the Senate issued a report.

At 3:45 a.m. on the morning of the vote, the final bill reached print. Legislators had to vote thumbs-up or thumbs-down, with no chance for further amendment. The assumption was that if the intelligence community had known about the 9/11 plot, it could have prevented it. Congress was keen to give the executive branch access to more information so it could better respond to future threats.

The legislation, which numbered hundreds of pages, made a slew of substantive changes, not only altering the Foreign Intelligence Surveillance Act of 1978 (FISA), but also introducing "delayed-notice search warrants" (allowing for the secret searches of premises) and extending the application of National Security Letters—a form of administrative subpoena, which could be used to bypass prior judicial approval and to obtain significant amounts of third-party information. These alterations broadened the amount of data the government could access. They chipped away at the particularity previously required before the government could collect citizens' information. And they muddied the distinction between foreign intelligence and criminal law, making it easier for the government to circumvent the protections of individual rights otherwise required by the Fourth Amendment.

The administration did not wait, though, for the legislature to pass new measures before it initiated new intelligence-gathering programs. Despite Congress's clear statement that FISA was to be the sole means via which domestic electronic surveillance for foreign intelligence purposes could be conducted, President George

W. Bush went outside the statute and directed the NSA to begin monitoring citizens' communications.

STELLAR WIND

On October 4, 2001, the president authorized the NSA to collect two types of information en masse: telephony and Internet metadata, and telephone and Internet content. Within a month, the program, renewed thereafter at 30–60 day intervals, became operational. Initially given the temporary cover term STARBURST, in October 2001 the NSA assigned a permanent cover term: STELLAR WIND. The mass surveillance program was emblematic of the new technologies available.

Metadata largely consists of information that describes who is communicating; potentially where they are located; the origin, path, and destination of each communication; and the length of the exchange. The purpose of collecting it was to give the government the ability to identify terrorist-related activity through social pattern analysis. An important part of the process is called "contact chaining," which is the process of building a graph that models communication patterns. Using this metadata, the administration could construct detailed pictures of society, such as who communicated with whom, which people were pivotal in relationships, and how important different individuals were to different groups and networks. The types of issues people cared about, the activities in which they engaged, how they spent their time in the digital sphere—all this could be learned.

Content, in contrast, refers to the actual words spoken—or written—in the course of a communication. The aim of content collection was to allow the government to sift through actual conversations, or communications, to identify and to monitor potential threats.

The costs of STELLAR WIND were relatively modest. It began with 50 computer servers to store and process data, with initial funding of just $25 million. From 2002 through 2006, the program cost $146 million.

The NSA built new structures to accommodate the program, creating a Metadata Analysis Center (MAC) in the Signals Intelligence Directorate. Within a month, it was fully operational. The FBI and CIA supplied telephone numbers, which the MAC could then immediately chain within the United States and with overseas signals intelligence. In October 2001, the private sector began sending telephony and Internet content. By the following month, NSA was receiving telephony and Internet metadata. Eventually, the project was consolidated into a new organization, the Advanced Analysis Division, which had three teams focused on Internet metadata, telephony metadata, and content. The FBI and CIA were co-located at the NSA to facilitate the program. Over the next five and a half years, around three thousand people—mostly NSA analysts—were cleared to work on the program.

The amount of information at stake was substantial. Millions of Americans' telephone and Internet metadata was collected and analyzed, and thousands of citizens' telephone numbers and e-mail addresses were targeted for content collection. According to a draft NSA report published by the Guardian in June 2013, the original authorization could be read to allow for domestic content collection even where both communicants were citizens located inside the United States.

STELLAR WIND was highly classified and entirely contained within the executive branch. Neither the American public nor Congress knew that citizens' telephony and Internet metadata, as well as the content of their telephone and Internet communications, were being collected, searched, and analyzed. No court formally approved the program. There was no external oversight.

To the extent that the legal basis of the program was assessed, it was done so inside the executive office—which largely approved of its own actions. For the first few years, even the NSA was not allowed to read the Office of Legal Counsel's (OLC) assessment of the legal grounds for the program, which had been provided to the president and vice president. At that time, some attorneys at OLC had an anomalous and expansive vision of executive power—a perspective that has since been repudiated not just by scholars and the public, but also by OLC itself.

The first internal objection came just after John Yoo, who had authored the memos providing legal support for the program, left government. STELLAR WIND was due to expire on March 11, so in early 2004 OLC initiated a reevaluation of the program. The attorney general would have to sign off on the collection for it to continue. Jack Goldsmith, appointed head of OLC in October 2003, later noted that he first encountered the program in 2003–2004, "long after it had been integrated into the post-9/11 counterterrorism architecture." He considered the challenge that he faced—"putting it legally aright," without destroying some of the most important tools available to government—as "by far the hardest challenge" he faced.[1]

OLC had concerns about the legality of the Internet metadata acquisition. The Department of Justice (DOJ) concurred. A week before the deadline, Deputy Attorney General James Comey met with Attorney General John Ashcroft and agreed that DOJ could not sign off on the program as it was being run. Shortly afterwards, the attorney general contracted pancreatitis and on March 4 was rushed to George Washington Hospital. James Comey became acting attorney general. Over the next week, he contacted the White House to let them know that DOJ would not agree to renew the program. The department's refusal led to an infamous showdown at the hospital bedside of Attorney General Ashcroft.

On March 10, 2004, Comey's security detail was driving him home when Comey received a call from the attorney general's chief of staff, telling him that Mrs. Ashcroft had just telephoned. White House Chief of Staff Andrew Card and Alberto Gonzales were on their way to the hospital to see her husband.

Comey hung up and immediately called his chief of staff, directing him to assemble as many people as possible at the hospital. He instructed his security detail to take him to the hospital. They turned on the emergency equipment and raced through the streets. Upon his arrival, Comey ran up the stairs to try to get to Ashcroft before the White House could force him to agree to extend the program. Jack Goldsmith, the head of the OLC, and Patrick Philbin, one of Comey's senior staff members, joined him. Comey took an armchair next to the head of the bed, with the other two DOJ representatives standing behind him. Mrs. Ashcroft stood next to the bed, holding her husband's arm. And they waited.

A few minutes later, the door opened, and Gonzales and Card entered. Gonzales carried an envelope. He greeted the attorney general and asked him to approve the program. Ashcroft, despite being very ill, lifted his head and refused, before noting that his opinion was of no consequence because Comey was the acting attorney general. Gonzales and Card turned and left.

Shortly afterwards, Card telephoned Comey and requested that he come to the White House. Comey refused to come without a witness present. He named Ted Olson, the solicitor general, as his second. Olson, who was at a dinner party at the time, hastily left and met Comey at DOJ, along with the senior leadership of the department. Olson and Comey then went to the White House, where they met with Gonzales and Card and reiterated their position.

The next day, the president signed the authorization without DOJ's support. Comey, Philbin, and Ashcroft's chief of staff all prepared to resign. Comey agreed to wait until the attorney general was well enough to add his letter of resignation to the pile. Monday, March 15, 2004, would be the day.

On Friday, March 12, 2004—what was to be Comey's last day as acting attorney general—President Bush asked to meet with him, and with FBI Director Robert Mueller, individually. At the conclusion of the meetings, the president changed course and ordered the programs either to be discontinued or moved to a statutory footing.[2]

Administration officials subsequently found what they considered an acceptable solution. They shifted the Internet metadata program to the pen registers/trap-and-trace authorities in FISA—the provisions that authorized the government to record the numbers dialed from, and the numbers calling, particular telephone numbers. The shift expanded the pen/trap provisions to apply to Internet communications. It was an extraordinary and unwarranted change, not least because FISA previously required particularized targeting *prior* to collection, whereas what was issued was a blanket order, allowing for widespread surveillance. The bulk order heralded a new age.

Once the Internet metadata program had been excised from STELLARWIND, Goldsmith approved of the three remaining programs (bulk telephony metadata, and the contents of international telephone and Internet communications), even though they operated outside of FISA (which explicitly forbade collection of electronic communications outside of the statute's remit), and lacked the particularity otherwise required under the statute. In May 2004, he issued a memo to the attorney general, claiming that, "in the circumstances of the current armed conflict with al Qaeda, the restrictions set out in FISA" amounted to "an unconstitutional infringement" of the president's powers. In Goldsmith's view, "The president has inherent constitutional authority as commander in chief and sole organ for the nation in foreign affairs to conduct warrantless surveillance of enemy forces for intelligence purposes to detect and disrupt armed attacks on the United States. Congress does not have the power to restrict that authority."[3]

The three remaining programs reviewed by OLC were known only to a small number of people. It was not until a *New York Times* article was published in December 2005—four years after the programs had been created—that their existence reached the public domain. At first, only a narrow portion emerged: the NSA's interception of some telephone content between the United States and overseas. Months later, the media reported further on the collection of domestic telephony metadata.

Congress, outraged, reiterated its statement from the 1970s that FISA was to be the sole means by which the executive branch could conduct electronic surveillance or run pen/trap devices for foreign intelligence collected within the United States. It was for this reason that Congress had included in the statute a clause that expressly contemplated the advent of war, allowing a 15-day emergency period, at the expiration of which the statute's provisions, if not formally amended by the legislature, would be in effect. While the 2001 Authorization for the Use of Military Force (AUMF) gave the president the authority to "use all necessary and appropriate force against those nations, organizations, or persons he determines planned, authorized, committed, or aided the terrorist attacks," neither the legislative history nor the text referred to electronic surveillance. Congress and the courts, moreover, had previously considered and declined to recognize claims to Article II authority to conduct foreign intelligence gathering inside the United States absent a warrant. This had been the basis on which FISA had been enacted.

In the face of mounting public pressure about what was then known about the program, the administration began to seek new powers under FISA to allow it to continue collecting international content. In the interim, in 2006 the NSA secretly transferred the remaining program, which collected telephone metadata, to a part of

FISA that the administration had managed to push through Congress in the wake of 9/11. The measure, which allowed the government to obtain "tangible goods" proved an ill fit, as the statutory language still did not support the breadth of the program already underway.

THE 2001 USA PATRIOT ACT

In the aftermath of the September 11 attacks, the intelligence community dismantled the restrictions previously placed on it in three critical ways. First, new measures expanded the type of information that could be obtained. Second, new (classified) legal interpretations helped to eliminate requirements that had previously anchored collection to particular individuals, replacing them with broad powers to obtain generalized information. Third, the changes muddied the distinction between foreign intelligence and criminal law. The iconic USA PATRIOT Act paved the way.

The pen register/trap-and-trace provisions provide a good example. Starting in October 2001, these devices could be used to obtain not just telephone numbers but *any* "dialing, routing, addressing, or signaling information" (referred to as "DRAS") that identified the destination or source of an electronic communication—including e-mail and Internet communications. Under pressure from the administration, in 2006, Congress further relaxed the statute, allowing the government to obtain subscriber records concerning *past* calls, as well as real-time information. The government may now use the pen/trap provisions to require electronic communication service providers to disclose the name, address, and telephone number of the customer or subscriber; how long the individual has been a customer; and the types of services the customer has utilized. Any records on the customer may also be requested, as well as records that detail the period of usage (or sessions) and any methods of payment—including the numbers of any associated credit cards or bank accounts.

In 2001, Congress also relaxed the requirement for factual proof prior to placement of a pen/trap device. Where previously the government had to demonstrate why it believed that a telephone line would be used by an individual engaged in international terrorism, after the USA PATRIOT Act, the government need only demonstrate that the information likely to be obtained does not directly concern a U.S. citizen and will be relevant to protect against international terrorism. In 2004, the administration used the enhanced pen/trap provisions, and a generous interpretation of the statutory language, as legal justification for the collection of Internet metadata. Hotly contested by civil libertarians, this provision was scheduled to sunset in December 2005, but Congress made it permanent.

Section 215 of the USA PATRIOT Act further expanded the types of information that could be obtained under FISA with regard to business records. Where previously the statute only allowed documents to be gathered from common carriers, public accommodation facilities, storage facilities, and rental car companies—already a significant amount of information—the new language authorized the FBI to apply for an order from the Foreign Intelligence Surveillance Court (FISC), "requiring the production of *any* tangible things (including books, records, papers, documents, and other items)."[4] In short, the government could acquire *any* business or personal record. Congress also eliminated restrictions on the types of businesses or entities on which such an order could be served. This meant that orders could be served on Internet service providers (ISPs), grocery stores, libraries, booksellers, hotels, universities, and pharmacies—just about any institution or company. The government quickly interpreted this to mean not just U.S. entities, but any company with an office within domestic bounds, as well as any data in the company's "possession, custody, or control," even if it is stored outside the United States.

The legislation removed the requirement that the FBI demonstrate "specific and articulable facts" indicating that the target of the search was a foreign power or an agent of a foreign power. Instead, it merely required that the government state that the "records concerned are sought for an authorized investigation ... to protect against international terrorism or clandestine intelligence activities," at which point the court became *required* to grant the order. The elimination of the link between the records and the target of the investigation meant that the government could collect information on people not suspected of wrongdoing, as long as it *related* to an authorized investigation.

What constitutes an investigation is within the domain of the executive branch—a definition that Attorney General John Ashcroft expanded. For the first two years, the guidelines allowed business record requests only as part of full field investigations. But in 2003, the attorney general authorized agents to obtain business records even during preliminary investigations.

As the authorities increased and particularization eroded, a further transformation in the overall framing occurred. Foreign intelligence and criminal law began converging, with the result that the weaker standards traditionally allowed in the national security began bleeding over into criminal law.

NATIONAL SECURITY AND CRIMINAL LAW CONVERGE

One of the first signs of convergence came in the demise of what is referred to as the FISA "wall." Until 9/11, a set of common understandings, practices, and regulations had erected a barrier, of sorts, between intelligence officials and law enforcement, preventing the free flow of information between the different types of government interests. This wall protected citizens' privacy by ensuring that law enforcement could not use the weaker standards in the foreign intelligence realm to target individuals for criminal prosecution, where the higher standards required under the Fourth Amendment prevailed.

The wall stemmed from an espionage case from the late 1970s involving a Vietnamese citizen, David Truong, who had moved to the United States in 1965. Eleven years after his arrival, he met Dung Krall, who was married to a U.S. Naval officer and had extensive contacts in France. During the 1977 Paris negotiations between Vietnam and the United States, Truong asked Krall (who, unbeknownst to Truong, was a CIA informant), to carry classified documents to Paris for the Socialist Republic of Vietnam. Warrantless surveillance revealed that Truong was receiving the materials from Ronald Humphrey, an American working at the United States' Information Agency. Truong and Humphrey were convicted of spying, as well as acting as agents of a foreign government without prior notification to the secretary of state.

The federal court of appeals suggested that there was a domestic foreign intelligence exception to the warrant requirement, so long as the investigation was focused primarily on foreign intelligence. At the point where the investigation turned *criminal* in nature, however, any information obtained without a warrant could be suppressed.

Although the court's decision was superseded by FISA, it led to what is referred to as the "primary purpose" test: as long as the primary purpose of the investigation was related to foreign intelligence, FISA could be used to collect information. In 1995, DOJ cemented this understanding into its regulations. Because investigators consistently followed this approach, no federal court ever had the occasion to suppress evidence in a criminal context because the investigation had not centered on foreign intelligence gathering. Courts, in turn, routinely recognized the validity of the primary purpose standard.

The rationale behind the wall was to prevent FISA from being used in lieu of ordinary criminal procedures. The point of having lowered standards was to facilitate the collection of information about significant threats to national security. Allowing the same for ordinary criminal law would amount to an end-run around Fourth Amendment requirements. The wall therefore prevented prosecutors from being able to use FISA to target individuals without first demonstrating probable cause that a crime had been, was being, or was about to be committed.

In 2000, the FISC issued a new rule reinforcing the wall. Any FBI officials who obtained information through FISA had to sign a document noting that they understood the requirement that they were not allowed to communicate across the wall without regulation from DOJ's Office of Intelligence Policy Review (OIPR)—in essence, recognizing OIPR's gatekeeping function. The court's instruction grated on the intelligence community.

The USA PATRIOT Act brought down the wall by altering the requirement in FISA that a government official certify that "the" purpose of collection was to obtain foreign intelligence, to read that it be "a significant" purpose. Senator Dianne Feinstein later explained that the change was necessary to take account of an increasingly complex world. "In many cases," she said, "surveillance will have two key goals—the gathering of foreign intelligence, and the gathering of evidence for a criminal prosecution. Determining which purpose is the 'primary' purpose of the investigation can be difficult, and will only become more so as we coordinate our intelligence and law enforcement efforts in the war against terror."[5]

Following the legislative changes, DOJ rewrote its regulations and submitted them to FISC for review. For the first time in the history of the court, FISC struck down DOJ's proposed language. The court recounted why the wall had been erected and suggested that the procedures appeared to be designed to substitute FISA for ordinary criminal searches. By removing the wall, "criminal prosecutors will tell the FBI when to use FISA (perhaps when they lack probable cause for a Title III electronic surveillance), what techniques to use, what information to look for, what information to keep as evidence, and when use of FISA can cease because there is enough evidence to arrest and prosecute."[6] Such measures did not appear to be reasonably designed "to obtain, produce, or disseminate foreign intelligence information," as required by the statute. FISC imposed conditions, drafted new provisions for DOJ, and required that OIPR be present at all meetings between intelligence and law enforcement. In a second first, FISC publicly released its opinion, leading to a third first: the government appealed.

The Foreign Intelligence Surveillance Court of Review (FISCR) overturned the lower court's decision. It objected to the lower court's effort to rewrite the executive branch's procedures. FISCR considered the primary purpose test arbitrary (as the government may have more than one purpose in conducting surveillance), and difficult to administer. The mere presence of law enforcement officers served as a proxy for intent—a proposition deeply problematic, since it prevented the government from benefiting from their expertise.

FISCR, though, went even further than either the USA PATRIOT Act or DOJ's proposed regulations. Not only could FISA information be used for ordinary criminal cases, but also the *primary* purpose of the investigation could be *criminal* in nature, "[s]o long as the government entertains a realistic option of dealing with the agent other than through criminal prosecution."[7] Stopping a conspiracy, for instance, would suffice. To reach this conclusion, the court rejected the Fourth Circuit court's finding in *United States v. Truong*.

The impact of the elimination of the primary purpose test is hard to ignore. Between 1978 and 1995, the executive annually made just over 500 FISA applications for electronic surveillance. In 2002, when DOJ issued its revised procedures, the number leaped to 1,228; and in 2003, to 1,727 applications. For the first time in history, the DOJ requested more wiretaps under FISA than under ordinary Title III wiretap statutes.

In the decade since then, the number of Title III warrant applications has plummeted, almost in direct proportion to the rise in FISA orders—suggesting that, as FISC predicted, law enforcement is turning to FISA, instead of Title III, to pursue ordinary criminal law cases.

To the extent that the foreign intelligence standards are weaker than those that are used in criminal law, the convergence matters. Both realms, for instance, require that the government establish probable cause prior to electronic surveillance. But what it applies to differs. Under Title III, the criminal standard, the court must find "on the basis of the facts submitted by the applicant that ... there is probable cause for belief that an individual is committing, has committed, or is about to commit" a particular offense.[8] FISA, in contrast, requires only probable cause that the target of electronic surveillance is a foreign power or an agent of a foreign power.

In criminal law, the government must establish, and the court must find, that "there is probable cause for belief that particular communications concerning [the specified predicate] offense will be obtained through [the] interception."[9] Nothing like this is required for FISA. The government need not demonstrate that foreign intelligence is likely to be obtained. Nor is it required to show that it was obtained prior to renewal. Instead, FISA relies on a certification from a high-level official that the information being sought is related to foreign intelligence. And FISC's standard of review is low: when the target is a citizen, the court merely looks at the certification to see if any clear error has occurred. Otherwise, there is no review.

Myriad other differences related to duration, notification, minimization, and sealing requirements distinguish the two realms. Allowing the government to use FISA in place of Title III empowers law enforcement to avoid restrictions that protect individual rights.

THE 2007 PROTECT AMERICA ACT

In December 2005, the *New York Times* article revealing portions of STELLAR WIND hit the public sphere. Political pressure increased on the administration. The attorney general responded by sending a five-page missive to congressional leaders justifying the program. The problem, according to the letter, was that FISA lacked the flexibility needed to identify potential threats.

At the time that Alberto Gonzales wrote the letter, Internet metadata collection had already been transferred to FISA's pen/trap provisions. Within six months, the NSA transferred the bulk collection of telephony metadata to FISA's Section 501 "tangible things" provisions (as amended by USA PATRIOT Act Section 215). The remaining collection programs, focused on *content*, proved more troublesome. To shift them to FISA, the government would have to find a legal theory to support the NSA's addition and withdrawal of thousands of foreign targets.

The immediate solution appears to have turned on a new definition for what constitutes the "facility" to be placed under surveillance. From being understood in its traditional sense—as a *particular* telephone number—DOJ began to interpret it to mean a cable head, or gateway—thus encompassing entire servers at telecommunications service providers' facilities. This understanding, which FISC eventually accepted, exponentially increased the amount of information that could be collected. Instead of just seizing or monitoring the content carried by a single telephone line, or to and from a particular computer address, the government could monitor and obtain the content of *all* telephone calls or Internet content run through telecommunication companies' routers.

Statutory changes swiftly followed. In April 2007, the Director of National Intelligence, J. M. McConnell, submitted a proposal to Congress to amend FISA to make it easier for the executive branch to target U.S. interests abroad. Four months later, Congress passed the Protect America Act (PAA), easing restrictions on the surveillance of foreigners where one (or both) parties were located overseas. In doing so, the PAA removed such communications from FISA's definition of "electronic surveillance," narrowing the term to include only domestic communications. The attendant restrictions, such as those related to probable cause that the target be a foreign power or an agent thereof, or likely to use the facilities to be placed under surveillance, or specifications related to the facility in question, dropped away.

The PAA prevented the court from supervising the interception of communications that began or ended in a foreign country (outside of the international communications of individuals targeted under traditional FISA for surveillance). Instead, the attorney general and the Director of National Intelligence could authorize, for up to one year, the acquisition of communications "directed at" persons reasonably believed to be outside the United States.

What these changes meant was that it became easier to establish that a target was located outside the United States. No individualized showing to FISC was required. Instead, the presence of reasonable procedures to ascertain location sufficed. Whether or not an individual could be placed under surveillance turned on geography, not on whether the target was a foreign power, or an agent of a foreign power, as was previously required by FISA for electronic surveillance as defined under FISA.

The PAA required the attorney general to submit targeting procedures to FISC and to certify that the communications to be intercepted were not purely domestic in nature. Once certified, the judges' hands were tied: the court was *required* to grant the order. The statute gave immunity to service providers for providing information, facilities, or assistance to the government in its exercise of authority under the PAA.

Intended to operate for six months, the PAA expired in February 2008, when the executive and legislative branches reached an impasse over whether retroactive immunity should be extended to businesses implicated in STELLAR WIND—a program widely regarded as illegal and unconstitutional. Cases attempting to hold private industry responsible began to make their way through the courts.

THE 2008 FISA AMENDMENTS ACT

After months of deadlock, Congress agreed to provide telecommunications companies with blanket, retroactive immunity for their participation in the program. The 2008 FISA Amendments Act (FAA) was hailed as a bipartisan solution to the tension among new and emerging technology, civil rights, and national security concerns. The legislation mostly weakened—although in some ways, strengthened—protections for citizens' international communications.

Section 702 of the FAA focused on the collection of electronic communications, where the target of the communications is not known to be a U.S. citizen and is believed to be located outside the United States. The argument for adding this section was strong. It centered on the nature of e-mail communications.

In 1978, Congress exempted foreign-to-foreign wire communications from FISA's remit. The exclusion made sense. The voice transmission of a British subject in London calling a French citizen in Paris at no point crossed U.S. borders. It would be impractical and cumbersome to expect the intelligence community to obtain court approval for every interception between foreign nationals overseas. By grounding the exception in territorial limits, Congress acted consistently with Fourth Amendment doctrine—reserving, in the process, the potential to act where citizens' privacy was more likely to be at stake.

In the modern age of e-mail, however, communications previously exempted from FISA had begun to fall within the statute, triggering the FISC approval process. U.S. ISPs, for instance, often stored foreign-to-foreign e-mail on domestic servers. If the same British subject accessed her e-mail from London (pulling it from a server within the United States), it suddenly fell within FISA—even when the e-mail she was retrieving was sent by a French citizen in Paris.

In other words, merely by using an American ISP, noncitizens could obtain the protections of the more rights-protective FISA framework—even where such persons had no other ties to the country and would otherwise be covered by the less rigorous contours of Executive Order 12333. Exacerbating the problem was the difficulty of determining where the user was located—inside the United States or on foreign soil—a consideration crucial to determining whether the intelligence community must first approach FISC for an order.

To deal with this problem, the FAA empowered the attorney general and the Director of National Intelligence jointly to authorize, for up to one year, the targeting of noncitizens reasonably believed to be located outside the United States. The law made it illegal for the NSA to engage in reverse targeting—that is, targeting someone outside the United States with the aim of obtaining the communications of someone inside the country. It also prohibited the NSA from obtaining wholly domestic communications. The agency may use Section 702 only when the target is believed to be outside the United States. The attorney general and Director of National Intelligence must attest that "a significant purpose" of the acquisition is to obtain foreign intelligence.[10] Congress limited the role FISC can play with regard to reviewing the certification, as well as the targeting and minimization procedures. As long as the certification elements are present, and the targeting and minimization procedures are approved, the court is *required* to enter an order authorizing the acquisition.

The FAA created an opportunity for companies served with orders to challenge the request. FISC may grant a petition, though, only where the request submitted to the company is unlawful. Otherwise, the electronic communication service provider must provide the requested information or risk being held in contempt of court. Either party may appeal to FISCR, with final review by the Supreme Court.

Section 702 of the FAA focused on the targeting of *non-U.S. persons* abroad. Sections 703 and 704 addressed the targeting of *U.S. citizens* outside of the United States for electronic surveillance and other types of acquisitions. By incorporating these provisions into the statute, Congress departed from previous practice, where the targeting of all persons overseas had been conducted consistent with Executive Order 12333, thus providing new and stronger protections for citizens.

Section 704 prohibits the intelligence community from targeting a citizen who is reasonably believed to be outside the country unless FISC or another provision in FISA authorizes it to do so. The limit applies where the target of the surveillance has a reasonable expectation of privacy and, if the activity was conducted within the country for law enforcement purposes, a warrant would be required. What this means is that where the NSA *knows* that a U.S. person is located overseas, *and that person is the target of the intercept*, it may engage in electronic surveillance (as statutorily defined).

In passing the 2008 FAA, Congress again emphasized that, as a constitutional matter, FISA was to be the *exclusive* means via which electronic surveillance could be conducted. California Representative Jane Harman, the ranking member of the House Permanent Select Committee on Intelligence (HPSCI) noted, "FISA is the exclusive means by which our government can conduct surveillance. In short, no more warrantless surveillance."[11] Representative Jim Langevin, a member of the HPSCI, stated, "FISA is the exclusive means by which the executive branch may conduct electronic surveillance on U.S. soil. No President will have the power to do an end-run around the legal requirements of FISA."[12] Wisconsin Senator Russ Feingold, who had served on the Foreign Relations, Judiciary, and Intelligence Committees, put the point most strongly, incredulous that the Bush administration had introduced STELLAR WIND in the first place under an Article II claim, overriding "an absolutely clear, exclusive authority adopted by Congress pursuant to Justice Jackson's third tier of the test set out in his *Youngstown* opinion."[13]

PROGRAMMATIC COLLECTION

Almost immediately after passage of the FAA, members of Congress, scholars, and journalists began criticizing Section 702 because of the potential for the government to use the authorities to engage in programmatic surveillance: obtaining and analyzing massive amounts of data on an ongoing basis, and not as part of a particular investigation.

Part of the problem is that because of the nature of international information flows, it may be impossible to tell if an individual is located overseas or within domestic bounds. Equally concerning is the global nature of communications, which was the impetus behind the legislation in the first place. If entirely international communications can be routed through the United States because of how the Internet works, then entirely domestic communications can be routed internationally. In neither case does the individual engaged in the communication have control over the geographic route followed by the data. What this means is that a considerable amount of citizens' communications could become subject to monitoring under the new provisions. Constitutional challenges to the FAA quickly followed.

The legislation was set to expire at the end of 2012. By early February, James Clapper, the Director of National Intelligence, and Attorney General Eric Holder had informed congressional leaders that reauthorization of the FAA was "the top legislative priority of the national Intelligence Community." The administration credited the FAA with the production of "significant intelligence that is vital to protect the nation against international terrorism and other threats." Offering classified briefings and attaching an unclassified annex, Clapper and Holder wrote, "We are always considering whether there are changes that could be made to improve the law in a manner consistent with the privacy and civil liberties interests of Americans." But their "first priority" was "reauthorization of these authorities in their current form."[14]

When asked for how many American citizens' communications had been intercepted, the NSA could not provide a number. Senators with access to the classified materials tried to bring to the attention of the American public the way in which the authorities were being used. By the end of July 2012, more than a dozen senators had joined a letter to Director Clapper, expressing alarm "that the intelligence community has stated that 'it is not reasonably possible to identify the number of people located inside the

United States whose communications may have been reviewed' under the FAA."[15]

Congress nevertheless extended the temporary measures. On September 12, 2012, with minimal debate, the House voted to reauthorize the 2008 FISA Amendments Act 301-118.[16] The Senate passed the bill at the end of December, 73 to 23.[17] President Obama signed the law that extended the FAA until December 31, 2017.[18]

Six months later, the documents leaked by Edward Snowden forced Section 702 into the public discussion. The information that has since emerged demonstrates that the NSA is using the provision for programmatic collection, in the process sweeping in millions of Americans' communications. The impact on citizens' right to privacy is significant, as is the impact of the collection of metadata—a subject to which we turn in the next chapter.

CHAPTER TWO

...

Metadata

DEFENDERS OF THE bulk collection of citizens' Internet and telephony metadata often justify it on the grounds that metadata represents a limited intrusion on privacy.[1] It provides general information—such as who contacts whom, when this occurs, and the length of the communication. Because the actual written material, or the precise language of what is being communicated, is not included, the logic runs, the impact is minimal.

At best, this argument is misleading. It fails to convey what can be learned from metadata, the insight that it provides into our daily lives, and the level of intrusion that it represents. Data is content, but metadata provides the context for everything we do.[2] It can reveal the most intimate details of our lives. And it is far easier to sift through and to analyze than pure content. As NSA's former general counsel, Stewart Baker, explained, "Metadata absolutely tells you everything about somebody's life." He continued, "If you have enough metadata you don't really need content ... [It's] sort of embarrassing how predictable we are as human beings."[3] General

Michael Hayden, the former NSA and CIA director, put the point even more strongly: "We kill people based on metadata."[4]

Why is metadata so important? It offers breadth, depth, and consistency, allowing for more accurate descriptive and predictive analyses of who we are, what we have done, and what we are likely to do. During one telephone call to a credit card customer service line, the content may suggest a problem in the recent billing cycle. Repeated calls may signal unresolved financial difficulties.

Even single calls may yield insight. A study conducted by computer scientists at Stanford University found that "phone metadata is unambiguously sensitive," even when collected on just over five hundred people for a few months.[5] The scientists were able to infer a range of medical conditions and beliefs, based on telephone metadata. Calls to health services, financial services, pharmacies, clinics for sexually transmitted diseases, divorce lawyers, and religious organizations provide inferential information.

Patterns in calls can reveal even more. One participant in the Stanford study spoke at length with cardiologists at a major medical center, talked for a short time with a medical laboratory, received calls from a pharmacy, and telephoned a home reporting hotline for a medical device that is used to monitor cardiac arrhythmia. Another individual called a firearms store specializing in AR-15 semiautomatic rifles before telephoning customer service for a manufacturer that produces an AR-15 line. One person telephoned a home improvement store, a locksmith, a hydroponics dealer, and a head shop. Yet another person telephoned her sister and spoke to her at length. Two days later, she called Planned Parenthood. Two weeks later she telephoned the clinic a few times and then one month later called it a final time.

The metadata provided insight into the participants' heart conditions, gun purchases, cannabis cultivation, and decision to have an abortion. And it was just a small sample, over a short period, of a limited number of calls.

The ability to make extensive use of metadata is a product of the rapid development of new fields. Communication technologies have created digital platforms and built the potential for mass communication. Simultaneously, the Internet has eliminated geographic barriers and accelerated information sharing. Accordingly, over the past three decades, scientific publications centered on social network analytics have proliferated. The digitization of information and powerful advances in computing—including the advent of the cloud computing industry—mean that massive datasets can now be mined to generate new knowledge. These advances have radically expanded the insights that can be learned about how people behave. And whereas massive amounts of content may prove difficult to analyze, metadata provides valuable information in a shortened—and accessible—form.

Beyond its analyzable qualities, metadata has the advantage that it is accurate. Content can be misleading. Individuals can lie or speak in code. But at some level, metadata is not controlled by those generating it. You can try to hide your telephony metadata by changing your calling pattern, but the information is still being recorded and stored by your communication service provider. Metadata is a by-product of operating in a technological age. Unlike content, telephony metadata cannot be encrypted. So even if consumers wanted to masque it from external analysis, they would not be able to do so. Internet metadata can be altered through sophisticated use of proxy services, allowing users to connect online, without leaving traces to their identity. But even the most sophisticated anonymizers, like Tor, can be circumvented.[6]

ALTERING BEHAVIOR

Beyond the privacy intrusion involved in gleaning such information about individuals and groups, the capacity to engage in social network analytics creates power. If the Democratic Party leadership had access to the telephone records of the Republican Party, it could identify who the most powerful people are in the network and then find a way to either alter their behavior or to isolate the key actors from the rest of the network. The analytics could be used to disrupt political opposition, which could be accomplished in obvious ways—such as finding evidence of illegal activity or bringing criminal charges against key individuals in the network—or through more subtle ways, such as pressuring and shaping the surrounding network itself.

Over time, social scientists have realized that our relationships alter our perceptions and actions. The more we are in contact with others and the more intensive our interactions, the more susceptible we are to being influenced by them. Understanding where the high-intensity relationships are for an individual thus gives others insight into where to exert pressure to manipulate others to act in certain ways. Controlling such corridors, or pathways, across the board enhances the potential for social or political control.

The possibility of using social networks to accomplish political aims is not far-fetched: the U.S. government has already initiated programs based on social network analytics to try to gain control over other countries. In 2010 the U.S. government began creating a Cuban "Twitter" to gain control of the population and use the network to undermine the Cuban government. The program, called ZunZuneo (Cuban slang for the noise made by a hummingbird) began by tweeting innocuous content, such as soccer results, the latest music, and weather reports. Once the network reached a critical mass of subscribers, the objective was to begin inserting content to encourage "smart mobs," gatherings called at a moment's notice, to trigger a Cuban spring. The goal was to "renegotiate the balance of power between the state and society."[7]

Part of the reason why social networks offer such a rich opportunity is because they are continually evolving. They thus can be used to manipulate and to alter others' behavior. They offer insight into individuals' attributes—such as what they like (or don't like) to do—as well as into the nature of their connections with others. Does one person in the relationship provide advice or support? Do they trust or betray each other? Social network analytics provide the context for relationships.

Since 9/11, attention has been paid to how to use network analysis to respond to terrorist threats. One of the obvious conclusions reached is that it is difficult to obtain information about highly secretive organizations. Nevertheless, terrorist networks have to communicate. Monitoring global communication systems offers one way forward.

There are problems, however, with this approach. For one, it has not been particularly effective. Although the government initially credited the telephony metadata program with being a critical part of discovering and thwarting dozens of planned attacks, after congressional scrutiny it could point to only *one* instance where the government had been able to identify a terrorist. A cab driver in San Diego had sent money to an overseas terrorist organization. It was hardly a smoking gun: for two months, the FBI did nothing with the information.

Experts have come to the conclusion that, as tools go, metadata is not a particularly good one for uncovering terrorist plots. In 2008 the National Research Council of the Academies of Science published the results of a two-year study by some of the leading scholars in the country in computer science, data mining, behavioral science, terrorism, and law. "Modern data collection and analysis techniques," it found, "have had remarkable success in solving information-related problems in the commercial sector . . . But such highly automated tools and techniques cannot be easily applied to the much more difficult problem of detecting and preempting a terrorist attack, and success in doing so may not be possible at all."[8] The Privacy and Civil Liberties Board, after having been given broad access to the NSA's telephony metadata program, concluded that it "has not proven useful in identifying unknown terrorists or terrorist plots."[9] Instead, it corroborated information that had already been obtained elsewhere. Set against the potential dangers of allowing the government to collect such information, the board recommended that the program be discontinued.

Scholars who work on social network analysis of terrorist organizations have explained why metadata programs often do not work for counterterrorism. The method used by the government to mine the data—the so-called snowballing method, via which the government identifies a telephone number and then looks at the associated numbers and, from that, at the next round of associated numbers—is biased toward highly connected actors. But terrorist organizations often operate in cells. It is not the most connected that are likely to engage in violent activity, but those on the periphery. A parallel claim has been made about Islamist networks in particular, which is that they are relatively sparse social networks—a characteristic, again, tied to their cell-like structure. Terrorist incidents, moreover, are relatively rare.

Another problem with the metadata approach is that it is not just terrorists who need to communicate. Every person in the United States relies on communications networks to go about their daily lives. It would be difficult to live in today's world without access to a telephone or the Internet. Almost every American therefore finds their private lives swept up in the search. And unlike terrorist organizations, which may have sparse communication networks, citizens' social networks may be dense, generating much more—and more intimate—information about millions of law-abiding citizens. The cost is borne in individual liberty and inroads into privacy.

At least two bulk metadata collection programs have been introduced in the post-9/11 world. Neither is legal, and neither passes constitutional muster.

INTERNET METADATA

In July 2004, the Bush administration moved the collection of Internet metadata from STELLAR WIND to the sections of FISA authorizing the placement of pen registers and trap-and-trace devices to capture incoming and outgoing traffic. This program had been rejected as illegal by the Department of Justice and, after John Yoo's departure, the Office of Legal Counsel (OLC). As the new head of OLC, Jack Goldsmith had been trying to find a way to make it legal. But forcing it into the FISA framework amounted to hammering a square peg into a round hole.

In the first bulk order approving the program, FISC Judge Colleen Kollar-Kotelly determined that the collection of information in specified categories was consistent with the statutory definitions of pen registers and trap-and-trace devices, as well as with the Fourth Amendment. In doing so, the judge accepted the government's argument, made without opposing counsel, that *all* Internet metadata was "relevant" to terrorism investigations. "[T]he collection of both a huge volume and high percentage of unrelated communications" was necessary to identify a smaller number of germane communications.[10] Although all of the information collected might not (indeed, could not) be relevant to a threat, the database, as a whole, was pertinent. The court authorized NSA analysts to access the metadata in the form of queries based on validated "seed" accounts—that is, "Internet accounts for which there was a reasonable articulable suspicion that they were associated with a targeted international terrorist group."[11]

It would be difficult to overstate the gravity of Judge Kollar-Kotelly's classified ruling. It single-handedly moved pen registers and trap-and-trace devices from requiring particularity about targets *prior* to information being collected, to allowing the collection of information without any previous indication of threats to national security. In taking this position, the judge embraced the arguments put forward by the director of the NSA in the 1970s—and roundly *rejected* by Congress in the passage of the 1978 Foreign Intelligence Surveillance Act. The prevention of widespread collection absent particularized suspicion was one of the most important safeguards introduced by Congress to protect citizens' privacy.

The FISC decision also violated the statutory language of FISA, which focuses on singular collection. FISA authorizes the judge to issue "an order" authorizing or approving "the installation and use of a pen register or trap and trace device," with reference in the application to "the person who is the subject of the investigation."[12] The statute specifies a single individual, who is the target of the investigation—not all individuals, almost none of whom have any relationship to the target of a particular investigation. The judge did not address this statutory language in her order.

Nor did the judge consider FISA's standard of review as indicative of the scope of the court's authorities. According to the statute, as long as the government certifies that the information is relevant, the court is not allowed to inquire further into the level of relevance. But that is precisely what the court did by questioning whether there were reasonable grounds for the government to certify that the information was relevant. Specifically, the judge considered whether the collection of all Internet metadata would be "useful . . . to help identify and track terrorist operatives."[13] By putting all the data into one place, the NSA would more easily be able "to detect and identify the Foreign Powers and those individuals affiliated with them."[14] The "safeguards" offered by the government, in turn, would "ensure that the information collected will not be used for unrelated purposes."[15]

In other words, the court's analysis turned on whether bulk collection amounted to a reasonable balance between security and privacy, as well as whether it provided a useful way to identify terrorists. This approach brought the judiciary firmly into the realm of policy making. Quite apart from the inappropriateness of such a determination, the implications of the judge's decision were profound. This interpretation was so broad that it read the insertion of "relevant" out of the statute. If all Internet metadata was relevant, then what Internet metadata was irrelevant?

The absurd implications of the court's reasoning become clearer when one looks to ordinary criminal pen/trap-and-trace provisions. The same language is at issue. Upon application, "the court shall enter an ex parte order authorizing the installation and use of a pen register or trap and trace device" where the court finds that the government has certified that the information likely to be obtained "is relevant to an ongoing criminal investigation."[16] Surely Congress did not intend for any federal prosecutor to be able to obtain all telephony metadata in the United States. So how was an almost identical statute read in this way?

Over time, FISC drew from Judge Kollar-Kotelly's interpretation of the term "relevant" with regard to Internet metadata, to shoehorn the telephony metadata portion of STELLAR WIND into Section 215 of the USA PATRIOT Act. This set a disturbing precedent in a highly classified world, without any public knowledge of how the plain language of the statute was being interpreted behind closed doors.

The Internet metadata program continued until December 2011, when the government decided not to seek reauthorization. But documents released by Edward Snowden demonstrate that the NSA still collects and analyzes massive amounts of citizens' online metadata—suggesting that the program was not so much ended as re-created in a different form.

TELEPHONY METADATA

Like the Internet metadata program that was originally part of STELLAR WIND, the Bush administration eventually transferred telephony metadata collection to FISA. In May of 2006, FISC issued the first order requiring Verizon to turn over its customers' metadata to the NSA. The court approved similar applications for other major telecommunication service providers. Over the next nine years, FISC issued orders renewing the bulk telephony metadata collection program forty-one times.

The program collected what the government referred to as "comprehensive communications routing information" held by companies about their customers, "including, but not limited to, session identifying information (e.g., originating and terminating telephone number, International Mobile Subscriber Identity (IMSI) number, International Mobile Station Equipment Identity (IMEI) number, etc.)."[17] It obtained the trunk identifier for each call (indicating which local cell phone tower was used in the connection), telephone calling card numbers, and the time and duration of each call.

For nearly a decade, the government secretly collected the data, in bulk, twenty-four hours a day, seven days a week, and stored it for further analysis. The NSA fed it into a database, which could then be searched with an "identifier," referred to as a "seed." FISC required that the NSA determine whether it had reasonable, articulable suspicion that an identifier used to query the data was linked to a foreign terrorist organization before running it against the bulk set. The agency analyzed the data to ascertain subsequent-tier contacts, in steps known as "hops." In other words, if target A called persons B, C, and D, the NSA could then find out who B, C, and D called, and so on. In this way, the organization could build a comprehensive picture of communications and contact between people.

Initially, neither FISC nor the NSA limited the number of hops that could be undertaken. From 2009 to 2014, the NSA interpreted the primary order as authorizing the agency to retrieve information as many as three hops away from the initial identifier. In January 2014 the president announced that the NSA would limit queries to two hops. The government referred to this process as "automated chaining." The results could be queried further for foreign intelligence purposes. The information also could be forwarded to the FBI for additional uses, including for an application to intercept the content of individuals' communications.

The telephony metadata collection program remained classified for seven years, until a combination of leaks by Edward Snowden and Freedom of Information Act litigation forced key documents, describing the program, into the public domain.

The revelations ignited a storm of controversy. Within a week of the first article, a bipartisan group of thirteen senators requested that the recently reconstituted Privacy and Civil Liberties Oversight Board investigate and provide an unclassified report to ensure "that the public and the Congress can have a long overdue debate" about the impact of the program on citizens' privacy. The following week the board met with President Obama and senior staff at the White House, at which time the president requested that the board consider "where our counterterrorism efforts and our values come into tension." The Obama administration went on to issue statements, fact sheets, redacted FISC opinions, and even a White Paper, acknowledging the existence of the program and arguing that it was both legal and constitutional.

The Privacy and Civil Liberties Oversight Board disagreed. In January 2014 it issued its report on the telephony metadata program. Despite extensive meetings with high-ranking officials and members of the intelligence community, and access to classified materials, the board had not been able to identify "a single instance involving a threat to the United States in which the program made a concrete difference in the outcome of a counterterrorism investigation." Neither had the program, at any point, contributed "to the discovery of a previously unknown terrorist plot or the disruption of a terrorist attack."[18] In the meantime, the impact on privacy and civil liberties was severe. The board was alarmed by the shift in balance of power between citizens and the state, the potential for mission creep, and the chilling effect of such surveillance on free speech. It declared the program illegal.

The board was not alone in its condemnation. In August 2013, the president announced the creation of a Review Group on Intelligence and Communications Technologies. Reporting in December 2013, the board unanimously recommended an end to the metadata program. "[T]he current storage by the government of bulk meta-data creates potential risks to public trust, personal privacy, and civil liberty." The Review Board continued, "the government should not be permitted to collect and store mass, undigested, non-public personal information about U.S. persons for the purpose of enabling future queries and data-mining for foreign intelligence purposes."[19]

In early 2014, President Obama announced reforms to the Section 215 program to ensure that metadata could be queried only after the FISC found a "reasonable, articulable suspicion that the selection term is associated with an approved international terrorist organization," and to limit queries of the data collected to two hops instead of three. He indicated that metadata collection would end by March 2014. But the deadline came and went, and the program continued.

Members of Congress thereafter took the lead in Section 215 reform efforts. In December 2014, legislation, supported by the administration, stood poised to pass. But when the vote came, the USA Freedom Act, which would have ended bulk collection, failed to pass the Senate by two votes. The administration continued—and FISC reauthorized—the program. Nevertheless, within six months, two crucial developments spurred the end of bulk telephony collection.

First, in May 2015, the Second Circuit ruled in *ACLU v. Clapper* that the telephony program did not comport with the law. The court rejected the government's argument that "relevant" should be understood as anything potentially bearing upon, connected with, or pertinent to a specified subject matter. Almost *none* of the information obtained was demonstrably linked to an authorized investigation. To the contrary, the records detailed the daily interactions of millions of Americans unconnected to foreign powers. They included private and public interactions between senators, between members of the House of Representatives, and between judges and their chambers, as well as information about state and local officials. They included parents communicating with their children's teachers, and zookeepers arranging for the care of animals—interactions irrelevant to national security.

The second conjuncture was the approach of the deadline set by a sunset clause in the USA PATRIOT Act, under which the government's Section 215 authorities would expire, unless renewed, on June 1, 2015. Congress had three choices: to renew or extend Section 215, to amend it, or to allow the powers to lapse. In a last-minute scramble, civil liberties concerns proved sufficient to prevent either renewal or extension of Section 215. The powers lapsed as the Senate quarreled over whether to adopt the USA Freedom

Act previously passed by the House. In the end, the Senate agreed to the House version and on June 2, 2015, the president signed the USA Freedom Act into law.

The statute requires that any orders seeking tangible things include a specific term (such as one identifying a person, entity, account, address, or device), which the company on whom the order is served then uses to obtain the information requested. Applications to the court must include a statement of facts demonstrating reasonable grounds to believe that the records sought are relevant to an investigation, as well as facts giving rise to a reasonable, articulable suspicion that the selection term is associated with a foreign power or an agent of a foreign power. Once obtained, the records must be subject to minimization procedures to weed out any records that the government determines do not relate to foreign intelligence. The statute similarly reinforced the pen/trap provisions, emphasizing that orders approving them include a specific selection term as the grounds for selecting the telephone line or facility to be placed under surveillance.

The upshot of these changes is that the NSA now may not hold bulk metadata under either Section 215 or the pen/trap provisions. Instead, it must first approach FISC for an order targeting a specific person or entity, which it then presents to a telecommunications company to obtain the relevant data.

It would, nevertheless, be a mistake to rely on the USA Freedom Act as protection against bulk metadata collection. Government officials continue to voice arguments supporting bulk collection, claiming its necessity in an age of Big Data. And it is unlikely that the Internet and telephony metadata programs were the only ones underway. Seven hundred and fifty-one applications for orders under Section 215 were granted during 2005–2015. Omitting the 41 ascribed to the telephony program, that still leaves another 711 orders, which, under the government's definition of the statutory language, could have easily included texting metadata, financial metadata, and various other records. There is nothing in the statute that requires that this information be expunged.

The Snowden documents demonstrate, moreover, that the collection of Internet metadata is still being conducted under Section 702, albeit starting from the point of one-end-foreign communications. The changes instituted by Congress also do not reach other forms of surveillance addressed by Executive Order 12333—which may include bulk collection. The promise of technology can be hard to resist.

As a judicial matter, the courts have yet to rule definitively. Even as it determined that the telephony metadata program fell afoul of the statutory provisions, the Second Circuit made it clear that it was *not* addressing the constitutionality of bulk collection.

As massive as these programs have been, however, and may continue to be, they pale in comparison to the content collection transferred to FISA in the aftermath of 9/11.

CHAPTER THREE

. . .

Content

On June 6, 2013, the *Washington Post* and the *Guardian* captured public attention by reporting that the U.S. intelligence community was incidentally collecting large amounts of citizens' private information. The NSA and the FBI were "tapping directly into the central servers of nine leading U.S. Internet companies, extracting audio, video, photographs, e-mails, documents and connection logs that enable analysts to track a person's movements and contacts over time."[1]

The press published a series of PowerPoint slides attributed to the NSA, describing a program called PRISM. The title slide referred to it as the NSA's most-used signals intelligence facility. The documents explained that PRISM draws from Microsoft, Google, Yahoo!, Facebook, PalTalk, YouTube, Skype, AOL, and Apple—some of the largest communications providers—making the type of information that could be obtained substantial: e-mail, video and voice chat, videos, photos, stored data, VoIP, file transfers, video conferencing, notifications of target activity (for example, logins), and social networking data. The program started in 2007 with just one commercial partner, steadily expanding over the next five years. The total cost was $20 million per year. By 2011, most of the more than 250 million Internet communications obtained each year by the NSA under Section 702 of the FISA Amendments Act derived from PRISM.

A follow-up article two days later printed another slide depicting PRISM and "upstream" collection of communications on fiber cables and infrastructure ("[c]ollection directly from the servers of . . . U.S. Service Providers.").[2] Upstream interception allowed the NSA to acquire Internet communications "as they transit the 'internet backbone' facilities." The NSA could monitor all traffic crossing cables—not just information targeted at specific Internet Protocol (IP) addresses or telephone numbers. The potential yield was substantial. The network of undersea fiber optic cables carries 99 percent of all intercontinental data. In the first six months of 2011, the NSA acquired more than 13.25 million Internet transactions through its upstream collection. The program accounted for 80 percent of the communications collected by the NSA. The text of the PowerPoint slide urged analysts to use both PRISM and upstream collection to obtain information.

Within days of the releases, the intelligence community verified the programs. In August 2013 the Director of National Intelligence, James Clapper, offered further confirmation, noting that PRISM had been in operation since Congress had passed the 2008 FISA Amendments Act. He declassified eight documents, and by the end of the month, he had announced that the intelligence community would release the total number of Section 702 orders issued, and targets thereby affected, on an annual basis.

PRISM and upstream collection reflect the migration of the content portion of STELLAR WIND to the 2008 FISA framework. Recall the strong argument behind enactment of the statute: communications that ordinarily would have come within Executive Order 12333 had, by accident of how the Internet works, found themselves funneled through the United States and subject to the stricter provisions of FISA. In light of the need for intelligence agencies to have access to international communications to protect U.S. national security, some change was necessary.

The problem is that it is a two-way street. Not only do entirely foreign communications now traverse U.S. borders, but entirely domestic communications fly around the globe at the speed of light. Everything users do online involves packets of information. Every website, every e-mail, every transfer of documents takes the information involved and divides it up into small bundles. The packets contain information about the sender's IP address, the intended receiver's IP address, something that indicates how many packets the communication has been divvied up into, and what number in the chain is represented by the packet in question. Packet-switched networks ship this information to a common destination via the most expedient route—one that may, or may not, include the other packets of information contained in the message. If a roadblock or problem arises in the network, the packets can then be rerouted, to reach their final destination. Domestic messages, as a result, may be routed through international servers, if that is the most efficient route to the final destination. The advent of cloud computing, and the rapid movement of users' data between foreign and domestic servers, means that a significant amount of private data and correspondence also may cross multiple international borders—outside users' knowledge or control.

What this means is that the geographic assumptions that have historically undergirded greater privacy protections for citizens no longer hold. Even if the NSA applies a filter to try to eliminate communications that appear to be domestic, it may nevertheless monitor conversations within the United States, or file transfers conducted by corporations, because they are routed through foreign servers. Through no intent or design of the users, the message becomes subject to NSA surveillance.

In this context, the NSA's implementation of programmatic collection, and the scanning of not just traffic to or from a target but also "about" them, impacts citizens' privacy. The NSA also has interpreted the statute to assume that targets are foreign and overseas. While the arguments in favor of these programs may be sustained with regard to genuine foreign intelligence collection, they raise troubling questions to the extent that the data may be collected and used for other purposes—including ordinary criminal prosecution.

CONSTITUTIONAL FOUNDATION FOR SECTION 702

Non-U.S. citizens who lack a substantial connection to the United States are not protected by the Fourth Amendment. The case that established this proposition stems from January 1986, when Mexican police apprehended Rene Martin Verdugo-Urquidez, a Mexican citizen believed by the U.S. Drug Enforcement Agency (DEA) to be a leader of one of Mexico's most powerful drug trafficking organizations. For the previous two years, the Guadalajara Narcotics Cartel had waged war against the DEA, kidnapping, interrogating, torturing, and killing agents and informants. Mexican authorities transported Verdugo-Urquidez to the U.S. Border Patrol station in Calexico, California, where U.S. Marshals arrested him. One of the DEA agents assigned to the case arranged for Verdugo-Urquidez's Mexican residences in Mexicali and San Felipe to be searched, with the aim of uncovering evidence of his involvement in the cartel's illegal and violent activities. The director general of the Mexican Federal Judicial Police authorized the searches.

At trial, the defendant tried to suppress incriminating items found during the search on the grounds that American officials had failed to obtain a domestic warrant. The Supreme Court disagreed. Unlike the Fifth and Sixth Amendments, which grant certain privileges to anyone brought before a U.S. court, the Fourth Amendment's reach was limited to protecting "the people of the United States against arbitrary action by their own Government." Chief Justice Rehnquist, writing for the Court, explained, "[I]t was never suggested that the provision was intended to restrain the actions of the Federal Government against aliens outside of the United States territory."[3] Only individuals with a "substantial connection" to the United States could claim the protections of the clause. A lawful but involuntary presence failed to suffice.

Concurring in the judgment, Justice Kennedy reached the same conclusion, albeit via a different route. He agreed that no violation of the Fourth Amendment had occurred, but he found the scope of the language—the right of "the people"—to be irrelevant. For him, the clause underscored the importance of the right being expressed. It did not limit those to whom the right applied. The central question was the appropriate scope of the Fourth Amendment in the context of U.S. foreign interests. Practicality won the day. Kennedy noted how other countries have divergent traditions and institutions. "The absence of local judges or magistrates available to issue warrants, the differing and perhaps unascertainable conceptions of reasonableness and privacy that prevail abroad, and the need to cooperate with foreign officials" indicated that the Fourth Amendment applies in a different manner overseas than within domestic bounds.[4]

In light of *United States v. Verdugo-Urquidez*, as a matter of criminal law, non-U.S. citizens located outside the United States, who lack a substantial connection to the country, are not entitled to the protections of the Fourth Amendment. Even weaker standards hold for the collection of foreign intelligence. This is why the guidelines in Executive Order 12333 are sufficient for foreign-to-foreign overseas collection related to non-U.S. persons. It is also why, to the extent that President Obama tried to reassure the international community in 2014 that the United States would, in the future, take the privacy rights of noncitizens seriously, his position was one of policy—not law.

As a constitutional matter, the real problem comes when, in targeting noncitizens overseas, significant amounts of U.S. persons' information is monitored and collected. That is the world in which we now find ourselves.

TARGETING

In his first report on Section 702, the Director of National Intelligence indicated in June 2014 that there had been only one order issued under the authorities. However, that order included 89,138 targets. And collection has not been limited to communications sent or received by the targets themselves. In the absence of explicit statutory requirements, the NSA has interpreted the 2008 FAA to enable the agency to obtain information "about" targets. This means that the NSA monitors traffic, looking for references to the targets, or to "selectors" associated with the listed targets, such as telephone numbers, e-mail addresses, or URLs. The target does not have to be a participant for the communication to be collected. Leaked procedures show that the to, from, or "about" interpretation reaches across the board, although currently, the NSA states that it conducts "about" collection only for Internet traffic intercepted upstream.

The government's interpretation of the statutory language departs from how FISA traditionally worked. Previously, FISA required that the government establish probable cause that the individual being placed under surveillance would use a specific telephone line or cable. Conversations intercepted were sent or received by the target. In contrast, the agency now scans all traffic passing through one or more collection points, looking for communications that mention the target or a selector associated with the target (e.g., badguy@ISP.com). In doing so, the NSA does not just consider envelope information (messages in which the selector is sending, receiving, or copied on the communication). It monitors and obtains content. The volume collected based on the broad search of Internet traffic is substantial: by 2011, the NSA was acquiring approximately 26.5 million Internet transactions per year as part of its upstream collection.[5]

Some percentage of the communications being monitored is between individuals located within the United States. Additional collection of domestic conversations takes place through the NSA's intercept of what are called multi-communication transactions, or MCTs. An MCT is a bundle of different communications. For example, when a user logs on to e-mail and the server downloads new messages into an inbox, multiple messages may be loaded at once. If even one of the communications falls within the NSA's surveillance, then *all* of the communications bundled into the MCT are collected. So if one of the e-mails happens to mention a target or a selector associated with a target as part of the subject, then the NSA obtains a list of all of the e-mails.

The consequence is of import. The Foreign Intelligence Surveillance Court (FISC) estimated in 2011 that somewhere between 300,000 and 400,000 MCTs were being collected annually on the basis of "about" communication where the "active user" was not the target. So hundreds of thousands of communications were being collected that did not include the target as either the sender or the recipient of the communication. Again, some subset of these communications may be wholly domestic. As the Office of the Director of National Intelligence has explained, if the NSA is "targeting a foreign person, and that foreign person is in communication with a U.S. person, you can get all of that U.S. person's screenshot."[6]

Assumptions made by the NSA about the object of the surveillance have further expanded the amount of information obtained. Targeting procedures require analysts to make a determination regarding the location and the legal status (i.e., citizenship) of a potential target. Together, these are referred to as the "foreignness determination." If the target is a non-U.S. person believed to be overseas, then the less restrictive requirements in Section 702 suffice for collection. Two related interpretations have allowed the NSA to push the statutory limits. First is the assumption, having looked at the evidence available, that a target located outside the United States or in an unknown location is a foreigner, absent evidence to the contrary. Second, where the target is not *known* to be inside the United States, the NSA presumes that the target is located outside domestic borders. These assumptions tilt the deck in favor of allowing collection.

As a statutory matter, the 2008 FAA is largely silent about what level of due diligence is required before the NSA can make a foreignness determination. The leaked targeting procedures state that analysts may consult databases. They do not require it. (Once analysts do have information about the target, they apply a totality of the circumstances test to weigh which evidence proves most persuasive.) According to a 2012 declassified compliance report, after making a location determination, analysts are required to "document in the tasking database a citation to the information that led them to reasonably believe that a targeted person is located outside the United States."[7] The citation entered must include a reference to the source of the information. The inclusion of this information enables oversight personnel to review the information that led the analyst to his or her conclusion. Unlike the location determination, analysts are not required to document the basis for the citizenship assumption, which makes the decision difficult to review.

It is unclear the extent to which the statutory vagueness—and, by implication, the NSA's default assumptions—influence the scope of collection. As a practical matter, there may not be many cases in which the NSA lacks information about the target's identity. Some sort of information must be available to ascertain that the information to be collected is of foreign intelligence value. Precisely what level of information is sufficient, however, is not clear.

For cases in which the only information available is that of a selector, only two assumptions are possible. Either one presumes that the individual is foreign and thus commences acquisition, or one presumes that the target is a citizen and thus falls within Sections 703–704. If the individual is known to be outside the United States, under a rational basis standard, it is logical to assume that he or she is more likely to be a non-U.S. person. A higher percentage of individuals outside the United States, after all, are non-U.S. persons. But in order for this to hold, the NSA must know at the outset that the individual is outside the United States. The circularity of the assumptions adopted by the NSA thus matter.

As a matter of status and location, the default makes sense. Intelligence collection at the point of communication is a binary system. Failure to intercept the conversation may mean a (permanent) loss of the information. Under this approach, the argument runs, it is better to make the assumption and to collect the information, putting more emphasis on minimization, if a target is later found to be a citizen or located within domestic bounds.

Nevertheless, there are dangers of approaching intelligence collection in this manner. The structure creates a disincentive to ascertain the status or location of the target—one, in this case, reinforced by judicial fiat.

Once a foreignness determination is made, NSA analysts must ascertain "how, when, with whom, and where" the target communicates. From this, they identify "specific communications modes," obtaining identifiers linked to the target. For each selector, NSA analysts must determine the expected foreign intelligence information, as well as information that would lead one to conclude that the selector is associated with a non-U.S. person abroad.

The vagueness of what constitutes "foreign intelligence information" is of note. The targeting procedures include examples of factors that analysts might take into account in determining whether a selector will be likely to result in foreign intelligence information. But analysts are not required to document their reasoning. This means that decisions cannot be subjected to careful review.

CONGRESSIONAL INTENT

To what extent could legislators have foreseen that the NSA would engage in programmatic collection under Section 702? Certainly, in 2008, Congress anticipated that the intelligence community might *inadvertently* collect citizens' communications in the process of targeting aliens. For this reason, legislators inserted limits on collection and required that information about citizens be minimized. But outside of a handful of exceptions, members of Congress did not publicly anticipate that the executive would engage in large-scale, programmatic collection. Legislators who did opposed the statute on those grounds. Not a single member who recognized the potential for programmatic surveillance defended the use of the authorities in this way.

To be fair, not all members of Congress appear to have understood the distinction between targeting citizens and collecting citizens' information as a *by-product* of targeting noncitizens. The confusion extended across party lines. Representative Heather Wilson, a Republican from New Mexico, for instance, lauded the legislation on the grounds that it would "protect the civil liberties of Americans and continue to require individualized warrants for anyone in the United States or American citizens anywhere in the world."[8] California Democrat Representative Anna Eshoo noted that "[T]he Administration would have to seek a court order before conducting surveillance on U.S. persons abroad."[9] At no point did either member acknowledge that at least some acquisition of citizens' communications could occur absent a court order, as long as the *target* was a noncitizen. Similar remarks characterize the debate in the Senate. Senator Benjamin Cardin, from Maryland, stated, "FISA requires the Government to seek an order or warrant from the FISA Court before conducting electronic surveillance that *may involve* U.S. persons."[10]

In two respects, though, the final legislation reflected an understanding that, at a minimum, in the process of targeting aliens, citizens' data might inadvertently be obtained.

First, the statute included minimization procedures that addressed how the executive branch would handle incidental data. Legislators looked to these provisions to discount potential privacy incursions. Second, Congress expressly prohibited the acquisition of purely domestic communications, the targeting of persons within the United States, and reverse targeting. The purpose was to ensure that the NSA did not use foreign targeting to collect information on citizens. The statute required the attorney general to adopt guidelines to ensure compliance with these limitations.

Some legislators did express concern that the authorities might be used on a massive scale, in the process collecting significant amounts of citizens' information. Without exception, these legislators opposed the final bill. Texas Representative Sheila Jackson Lee railed that the compromise bill "fail[ed] to protect American civil liberties both at home and abroad." She explained, "[The bill] permits the Government to conduct mass, untargeted surveillance of all communications, coming into and out of the United States, without any individualized review, and without any finding of wrongdoing."[11] Representative Bobby Scott, a Democrat from Virginia, noted, "The bill actually permits the government to perform mass untargeted surveillance of any and all conversations believed to be coming into and out of the United States without any individualized finding and without a requirement that wrongdoing is believed to be involved at all."[12] California Representative Jackie Speier's statement proved prescient. "It is fundamentally untrue to say that Americans will not be placed under surveillance," she stated. "The truth is, any American will subject their phone and e-mail conversations to the broad government surveillance web simply by calling a son or daughter studying abroad, sending an email to a foreign relative, even calling an American company whose customer service center is located overseas."[13]

These and other, similar statements stood in sharp contrast to the legislators who supported the bill, *all* of whom discounted the amount and extent of incidental information that might be obtained, pointing to the minimization procedures as a way to address any privacy concerns. Senator Cardin summarized, "The legislation provides for the inspector general to review the targeting and minimization provisions. The targeting is when a U.S. citizen, perhaps indirectly, is targeted. And the minimization procedures deal with when the intelligence community gets information about an American without court approval, to minimize the use of that information or to seek court approval."[14] Notably, Cardin anticipated the potential interception of communications of *an* American—not the monitoring of *all* Americans engaged in international communications. He cabined the amount of data ("that information"), and stated that the minimization procedures would further protect the information obtained. Senator

Christopher "Kit" Bond similarly discounted the potential for programmatic surveillance, stating, "The bugaboo that this [bill] gives the intelligence community the right to listen in on ordinary citizens' conversations willy-nilly, without any limitations, is absolutely false. That is why we built in the protections in the law. That is why we have the layers of supervision to make sure it does not happen."[15]

ACQUIESCENCE

Even if Congress did not realize what it was authorizing in 2008, the intelligence community kept the legislature informed about the programs underway. At a minimum, therefore, at the point of reauthorization in 2012, Congress agreed to programmatic surveillance. To the extent that Congress later cried foul, the fault appears to be of its own making.

The 2008 FAA requires that the administration inform the intelligence committees and the Committees on the Judiciary of the Senate and the House of Representatives about how the Section 702 authorities have been used, including any significant legal interpretations. The intelligence community did so. Its (classified) May 2012 report, which detailed PRISM and upstream collection, was made available to Congress more than a year before the Snowden revelations. Nevertheless, many legislators voted for renewal *without reading the materials*. Congressional leadership appears to have actively prevented 93 junior members, who had not been present during the enactment of the 2008 FAA, from seeing the reports on programmatic collection.[16]

One concern frequently voiced by legislators is that even if they have access to classified information, there is not a lot that can be done about it. This is a curious argument, as it seems to ignore the fact that they could simply vote "no" to renewing the authorities.

They could condition continuation of the authorities, or funding for the NSA, on curbing the programs. Congress did none of these things. The House did not hold a single hearing on how the law was operating, prior to voting on whether to renew the FAA.

It is true that the classified nature of surveillance complicates the discussion. But there are numerous ways around efforts by the executive to masque its activities from the public. If Congress had wanted to have a debate about the programs, or the secret legal interpretations that undergirded the collection of citizens' data, members could have read information into the public record. Legislators are constitutionally protected from any criminal or civil charges that can follow from anything said on the floor of Congress.

The Speech or Debate Clause in the U.S. Constitution states that legislators "shall not be questioned in any other Place" "for any Speech or Debate in either House." In 1971, Senator Mike Gravel used this clause to read portions of the *Pentagon Papers* on the floor of the Senate and then place all 47 volumes of the study into the *Congressional Record.* The Supreme Court subsequently found it "incontrovertible" that the clause, at a minimum, protects legislators "from criminal or civil liability and from questioning elsewhere than in the Senate, with respect to the events occurring" in the course of congressional hearings. Justice White, writing for the Court, explained, "The Speech or Debate Clause was designed to assure a co-equal branch of the government wide freedom of speech, debate, and deliberation without intimidation or threats from the executive branch. It thus protects Members against prosecutions that directly impinge upon or threaten the legislative process."[17]

Having read statements into the public record, senators may still risk congressional censure or being placed under investigation for a breach of ethics. But such actions are within the domain of the legislature, not the executive. To the extent that the argument against using the Speech or Debate Clause centers on the risk that the flow of information between the executive and Congress might be damaged, it rather begs the point: the threat of noncooperation unless the legislature plays ball amounts to bullying legislators into agreeing with the executive, at which point they have failed in one of their most basic constitutional responsibilities.

To be sure, there are logistical problems related to congressional access to classified information. To read the material, legislators must go a Sensitive Compartmented Information Facility, a room tucked away in the U.S. capitol, with limited access. Most members do not have staff cleared to read classified documents, so it must be the members themselves, whose time is cabined, who review the hundreds of pages of materials. They are not allowed to remove material from the facilities; nor are they allowed to take their notes with them. Everything must remain under lock and key. The result is that most legislators do not read the relevant materials and, therefore, remain, in Senator Wyden's words, "in the dark."[18]

While it may be difficult and time consuming to read the reports, it is Congress's job to provide oversight. The fault for its failure to do so lies squarely at the steps of the Capitol.

THE ROLE OF THE FOREIGN INTELLIGENCE SURVEILLANCE COURT

If some members of Congress abdicated their responsibility by failing to find out what was being done under legislation before they voted for renewal, the FISC, which was familiar with PRISM and upstream collection, did not hold the executive to account. It relied on the NSA to police itself and, when the NSA did not do so, it gave the agency a slap on the wrist and allowed it to continue collection. Further, although the statute prohibited the NSA from intentionally collecting wholly domestic conversations, even after the NSA *told* the Court that it had knowingly collected tens of thousands of wholly domestic conversations, the Court let the NSA continue collection.

FISC first became aware of the implications of the NSA's interpretation of to, from, or "about" collection three years after the administration transferred content collection to the FAA. The court was surprised by the government's admission that it would have to intercept significantly more content to scan it for relevant information. In its first Section 702 docket, the government had indicated that the acquisition of telephonic communications, "would be limited to 'to/from' communications—i.e., communications to or from" a target. According to the court, "The government explained . . . that the Internet communications acquired would include both to/from communications and 'about' communications—i.e., communications containing a reference to the name" of the target. The implications of the change had not been clear. FISC explained, "Based upon the government's descriptions of the proposed collection, the Court understood that the acquisition of Internet communications under Section 702 would be limited to discrete 'to/from' communications between or among individual account users and to 'about' communications falling within [redacted] specific categories that had been first described to the Court in prior proceedings." The court had not taken into account the NSA's acquisition of Internet transactions, which "materially and fundamentally alter[ed] the statutory and constitutional analysis."[19]

In 2011, FISC was troubled by the government's revelations—not least because it was the third time in less than three years in which the NSA had disclosed a "substantial misrepresentation" on "the scope of a major collection program."[20] Either the court lacked intellectual rigor, or the government had made repeated mistakes, or the government had been lying. Regardless, "[t]he government's submissions make clear not only that NSA has been acquiring Internet transactions *since before the Court's approval* of the first Section 702 certification in 2008, but also that NSA seeks to continue the collection of Internet transactions."[21] So the NSA had been collecting Internet transactions without judicial approval, entirely outside the FAA—and it sought to continue collection.

FISC noted that it is a crime to "engage[] in electronic surveillance under color of law except as authorized" by statute or . . . to "disclose[] or use[] information obtained under color of law by electronic surveillance, knowing or having reason to know that the information was obtained through electronic surveillance not authorized" by statute.[22] To the extent that multi-communication transactions contained communications that the NSA was not supposed to collect, the agency had acted outside the law.

So the NSA had engaged in illegal activity. The court acknowledged that it had been illegal. And nothing was done about it. Instead, FISC allowed collection to continue.

What made this decision even more remarkable is that the statute explicitly prohibited the knowing collection of domestic communications. The NSA acknowledged that it collected tens of thousands of domestic communications. Nevertheless, the court ruled the procedures compatible with the statute.

The court's reasoning centered on technology. The NSA's collection devices lacked the ability, at the time of acquisition, to distinguish between transactions containing only a single communication to, from, or about a target, and transactions containing multiple discrete communications, some of which had no relationship whatsoever to the target. "As a practical matter," the court wrote, "this means that NSA's upstream collection devices acquire any Internet transaction transiting the device if the transaction contains a targeted selector anywhere within it."[23] Because of the enormous volume of communications intercepted, it was impossible to know how many wholly domestic communications were thus acquired or the number of citizens' communications intercepted.

The way the court avoided a statutory violation was by noting that, because the equipment did not have the ability to distinguish between domestic and international communications, the NSA could not technically know, *at the time of collection*, where the communicants were located. From this, the court was "inexorably led to the conclusion that the targeting procedures are 'reasonably designed' to prevent the intentional acquisition of any communication as to which the sender and all intended recipients are known at the time of the acquisition to be located in the United States."[24] The NSA had circumvented the spirit but not the letter of the law.

Such decisions encourage a form of willful blindness. In brief, it is in the NSA's best interests not to develop the technologies necessary to minimize collection. By not doing so, agents have access to more information.

Stepping back, as a structural matter, it is possible to look at FISC's role in the collection program and to conclude that there is no problem. All three branches of government considered the authorities, and their implementation, and approved.

But there is another way this could be seen. One judge secretly approved the program. There was no review of the decision because there was no appeal. The executive, which got what it wanted, was hardly going to argue against the decision. And it was not Congress as a whole that performed oversight, but the 15 legislators on SSCI, some of whom expressed deep concern about how the powers were being used but were prevented from saying anything publicly. A small number of people were thus able to approve enormous inroads into the rights of the entire population. They were able to do so, in part, because of new powers, secret legal interpretations, and a lack of transparency.

SURVEILLANCE AND CONVERGENCE

When Congress enacted the 2008 FAA, it was concerned that the executive branch would use the authorities to engage in reverse targeting—that is, targeting individuals overseas, with the actual purpose of collecting information about individuals located within domestic bounds. Despite the legislature's concern, the NSA instituted (and FISC approved) a rule change in October 2011 to make it possible to query the content of communications obtained via PRISM and upstream collection using citizens' private information. If the intelligence community wants to query the data for information about citizens on the grounds that such queries are likely to yield foreign intelligence information, it may now do so. It is not required to ask any court for permission.

In March 2014, the Director of National Intelligence confirmed in a letter to Senator Ron Wyden that the NSA does query Section 702 data using U.S. person identifiers. Pressed during a June 2014 hearing for the number of queries, James Clapper revealed that in 2013, the NSA approved 198 U.S. person identifiers for querying the content of Section 702 communications, and that it queried Section-702-acquired metadata in this manner approximately 9,500 times.[25]

The rule change provides a good example of how intelligence gathering programs steadily expand. The procedures initially approved by FISC prohibited queries using citizens' information. But three years later, the government broadened its procedures to allow the NSA to do so, where such queries were "reasonably likely to yield foreign intelligence information." The court did not find the government's change of heart problematic. Because the initial collection of the information centered on noncitizens located outside the country, it would be less likely, in the aggregate, "to result in the acquisition of nonpublic information regarding non-consenting United States persons."[26]

The logic of this statement does not play out. If Section 702 is meant to intercept communications between the United States and overseas, then it is *highly likely* that at least one party to the communications will be a citizen. The content of the communications, moreover, is hardly public information. For the court's statement to be true, then the citizen at one end of the phone, or Internet connection, must be fully consenting to surveillance. The implication is that every U.S. citizen who communicates internationally consents in so doing to have the government monitor their conversations. This is an extraordinary proposition, not least because individuals may have no control over whether some of their communications are even routed overseas. So how could they "consent"?

As a practical matter, what this rule change means is that citizens' communications collected via Section 702 can now be mined using citizens' information as part of the queries. The practice appears inconsistent with Congress's requirements in Sections 703 and 704 that prior to citizens' information being obtained (and therefore before it is analyzed), the government must be required to appear before a court to justify placing a citizen under surveillance.

An even more serious consequence arises in the context of criminal law. The FBI stores unminimized Section 702 data together with information obtained from traditional FISA orders, allowing agents to search both caches of information simultaneously. FBI queries of Section 702 information may have nothing to do with threats to U.S. national security. The Privacy and Civil Liberties Oversight Board explained, "With some frequency, FBI personnel will . . . query [Section 702] . . . data . . . in the course of criminal investigations and assessments that are unrelated to national security efforts."[27] The Bureau does even not track the number of queries undertaken.

This practice highlights the convergence between criminal law and national security. Information obtained for foreign intelligence purposes can now be used for law enforcement—without the government ever establishing probable cause that an individual has committed, is committing, or is about to commit a crime, and without any particularized showing to a third-party magistrate, with evidence of criminal activity provided, under oath, by the accuser. This is not a minor concern. The cost is born by inroads into rights that we have long—and for good reason—protected.

CHAPTER FOUR

...

Origins of the Fourth Amendment

The Fourth Amendment prohibits the use of general warrants. The history on this point is incontrovertible.[1] The War of Independence was fought, in part, because of the Crown's effort to exercise writs of assistance—a form of general warrant wherein government officials failed to specify the person or place to be searched; or to provide evidence, under oath, to a magistrate, of a particular crime. James Otis's fiery oration in Boston against Britain's use of general warrants became a rallying cry for the colonists. "Then and there," John Adams wrote, "was the first scene of the first Act of Opposition to the arbitrary Claims of Great Britain. Then and there the child Independence was born."[2]

In their rejection of general warrants, the Founders were heavily influenced by English history and political thought. For centuries, legal scholars had considered promiscuous search and seizure a violation of the common law. General warrants were regarded as the worst exercise of tyrannical power.

Accordingly, state declarations of rights and constitutions uniformly rejected general warrants as a violation of individual rights. The only way that the government could intrude on the sanctity of one's home to search for contraband or the instruments of crime was by presenting evidence, under oath, to a magistrate, of a crime committed, and for the court to issue a warrant under its own seal, particularly describing the place to be searched and the individual on whom the warrant would be served. It was with the expectation that new language banning promiscuous search and seizure would be added to the Constitution that some of the most important states to join the Union ratified it.

In the post-9/11 world, general warrants have returned with a vengeance, giving rise to serious question about the constitutionality of the government's actions.

ENGLISH LAW

The rejection of general warrants boasts a pedigree that stems back to the 1215 Magna Carta. There could be no liberty if the Crown could search any subject's home without cause, seize his papers, and use them to construct charges of criminal activity. The sanctity of the home lay at the heart of the objection. As the Court of the King's Bench famously announced in 1604, "[T]he house of everyone is to him as his castle and fortress."[3] It could be breached only under limited circumstances.

Despite the principle, beginning with Henry VII, Englishmen increasingly found their homes entered and their papers and effects inspected at the Crown's pleasure. Having seized the monarchy from Richard III, Henry Tudor's claim to kingship was somewhat tenuous. He expanded his powers to head off threats to his government. His progeny went on to employ general searches to solidify social, political, economic, and intellectual control. In 1559, Elizabeth I created a High Commission, which was charged to "devise all . . . politic ways and means" to search out those who defied her rule. The Privy Council made use of general warrants, directing the queen's men to search any places suspected of housing papers contrary to state interests. James I expanded the High Commission's jurisdiction to include the power to search for papers considered seditious as well as heretical, and to target not just those writing such documents, but anyone who printed or distributed them. Shortly thereafter, he extended the commission's remit to include any materials "offensive to the state."

The increasing use of general warrants and their expansion to other areas of the law—ranging from the pursuit of individuals accused of crime and recovery of stolen possessions, to economic regulations, weapons, customs, and the suppression of political and religious ideas—meant that what had been an infrequent experience to which few people had been subjected became a common action to which many were exposed.

The English Civil War heralded the beginning of a systematic assault on general warrants. Its chief architect was Sir Edward Coke, whose *Institutes of the Laws of England* fundamentally transformed English legal thought. Coke was well qualified to comment. In addition to his formidable mastery (and manipulation) of English law, Coke had participated in the execution of one of the most notorious promiscuous searches of the times and had himself been subjected to a general warrant.

In 1605 James I responded to the Gunpowder Treason Plot, an ill-fated effort to assassinate the king, by issuing two general warrants directed toward apprehending individuals suspected of complicity. Coke, then attorney general, assisted in executing the warrants by searching the chambers of a Catholic family in the Inner Temple and seizing their books.[4]

Less than two decades later, Coke found himself at the receiving end of a general warrant. James I had him detained, while agents of the Crown searched his home and chambers. Ordered "to make diligent search for all such papers and writings as do in any way concern his Majesty's service" and "to open all such studies, closets, chests, trunks, desks, or boxes that you shall understand or probably conceive" contain such material, officers brought Coke's papers before the Privy Council.[5]

Coke cited this experience in Parliament to argue for the inclusion of clauses in the Petition of Right prohibiting promiscuous search and seizure. "I was committed to the Tower and all my books and study searched, and 37 manuscripts were taken away," he said. "I was inquired after what I had done all my life before. So then there may be cause found out after the commitment."[6] Coke went on to reject reason of state as sufficient grounds to justify a general warrant.

While other commentators had condemned the methods employed by the Crown to arrest individuals and to search their personal papers, it was Coke who recognized general warrants as the enabling device. "One or more justices of peace," he wrote, "cannot make a warrant upon a bare surmise to break any man's house to search for a Felon, or for stolen goods."[7] Evidence of the person's guilt in the acts alleged must be produced. To issue general warrants, he stated, "is against Magna Carta."[8] Claims must be demonstrated in open court, "because Justices of Peace are Judges of Record, and ought to proceed upon Record, and not upon surmises."[9] The 1628 English Petition of Right subsequently incorporated the illegality of general warrants.

Whatever one may think of Coke's somewhat generous interpretation of Magna Carta, his writing reflected growing frustration at the ever-expanding use of general warrants by the Crown. He grounded his rejection in the most ancient of English rights: the right to be secure in one's own home. It was not that general warrants were not in use. To the contrary, Coke himself acknowledged the frequency with which they were exercised. The issue was that they violated Magna Carta.

In a twist of fate, the *Institutes* fell subject to the very warrants they condemned. As Coke lay dying, Charles I ordered that his home be searched and "all such papers and manuscripts" as considered fit for confiscation be seized. The king himself broke open the trunks when they arrived and catalogued their contents.

Charles I's actions were too late to stem the tide. The *Institutes* were published and commentators went on to cement Coke's analysis into English thought. Sir Matthew Hale's *History of the Pleas of the Crown*, which appeared in 1736, stated, "[A] general warrant to search in all suspected places is not good, but only to search in such particular places, where the party assigns before the justice his suspicion and the probable cause whereof, for these warrants are judicial acts, and must be granted upon examination of the fact." General warrants, "are not justifiable, for it makes the party to be in effect the judge."[10]

It was to Coke and Hale that Sergeant William Hawkins appealed in his *Pleas of the Crown* to underscore the illegality of general warrants: "I do not find any good Authority, That a Justice can justify sending a general Warrant to search all suspected Houses in general for stolen Goods," he wrote.[11] Numerous influential legal treatises and abridgments followed, condemning general warrants.

In the light of legal scholarship, Parliament began to chip away at the edifice on which general warrants perched. In 1764 the House of Commons passed a Resolution condemning the use of general warrants for libels. The issue returned to the floor in January 1765. Members argued that if seizing authors, printers, and publishers for libel, sedition, or treason, under general warrant, was objectionable, use of the same "for seizing their papers was still more so." The potential for papers to be combined or disjoined, they observed, "so as to make of them engines capable of working the destruction of the most innocent persons" could not be ignored. Even particular warrants, without indicating the specific documents to be obtained, "may prove highly detrimental, since in that case, all a man's papers must be indiscriminately examined, and such examination may bring things to light which it may not concern the public to know, and which yet it may prove highly detrimental to the owner to have made public."[12]

By 1766, comment in Parliament had become even more extreme: "a general warrant is such a piece of nonsense as deserves not to be spoken of, being no warrant at all, and incapable of answering any on purpose, in any case whatever, that a legal warrant would not better attain."[13]

Influential English cases further laid the groundwork for the Founders' rejection of general warrants. In *Entick v. Carrington*, Charles Pratt, chief justice of the Court of Common Pleas, confronted the Crown's use of the writs to search for evidence of seditious libel. In ruling against the government, Pratt famously observed, "The great end, for which men enter[]into society [is] to secure their property." Under English law, "every invasion of private property, be it ever so minute, is a trespass." By this, Pratt did not mean physical intrusion: "Papers are the owner's goods and chattels: they are his dearest property; and are so far from enduring a seizure that they will hardly bear an inspection."[14] The power of issuing general warrants, "would be more pernicious to the innocent than useful."

By 1768, William Blackstone's *Commentaries on the Laws of England* announced that the question had been well settled: "Sir Edward Coke indeed hath laid it down, that a justice of the peace cannot issue a warrant to apprehend a felon upon bare suspicion; no, not even till an indictment be actually found." Blackstone underscored the distinction between *specific* and *general* warrants. The former may lead to arrest on the basis of individualized suspicion. Evidence must be submitted, under oath, to a competent judge, who may then issue a warrant for arrest. In contrast, "A *general* warrant to apprehend all persons suspected, without naming or particularly describing any person in special, is illegal and void for its uncertainty; for it is the duty of the magistrate, and ought not to be left to the officer, to judge of the ground of suspicion."[15]

By the time of the American Founding, English Law Lords, legal treatises, and Parliament had come to reject general warrants. In a few areas, such as customs, promiscuous search and seizure persisted, yet it was fraught with controversy—perhaps nowhere more so than in the American colonies. The increasing use of the associated instruments—writs of assistance—created ever-greater friction between colonists and the king, in much the same way that broader use of general warrants preceding the English Civil War had engendered a legal battle between English subjects and the Crown.

THE CHILD INDEPENDENCE

One of the most important incidents in the road to Independence was James Otis's oration in what is known as *Paxton's case.* It stemmed from actions taken on the eve of the French and Indian War. Massachusetts Bay Governor William Shirley decided to take action to prevent French Canada from benefiting from illegal commerce. Shirley drew on his executive, gubernatorial powers to direct his customs officers, among them Charles Paxton and Thomas Lechmere, to use writs of assistance to search the colonists' ships, warehouses, and homes for contraband.

In 1755, Paxton obtained word that a prominent Loyalist's brother had illegal goods stored in his Boston warehouse. When he went to the site to perform the search, the Loyalist,

Harvard-educated Thomas Hutchinson, challenged Paxton's authority. Paxton produced the governor's writ. Hutchinson retrieved the keys to the warehouse and gave them to the customs officer, but he strongly objected that the writ was not valid. The governor did not have the power to execute a general warrant on his own authority. He declared that Paxton could be sued for breaking and entering.

Paxton reported Hutchinson's remarks back to Governor Shirley, who directed the customs officers to get a judicial writ to replace the one that he had issued under his inherent executive power. Accordingly, Paxton submitted an application to the Massachusetts Bay Superior Court to obtain a writ of assistance to enable him to carry out his duties.

The court granted the petition, directing justices of the peace to allow Paxton and his deputies, "from Time to time at his or their Will as well in the day as in the Night to enter and go on board" any ship, boat, or vessel, "to View and search" and to examine the premises in the interests of obtaining customs and subsidies. The writ allowed customs officers in daytime "to enter and go into any Vaults, Cellars, Warehouses, shops or other Places to search and see, whether any Goods, Wares or Merchandizes, in the same ships, Boats or Vessels, Vaults, Cellars, Warehouses, shops or other Places are or shall be there hid or concealed," and, further, "to open any Trunks, Chests, Boxes ... or Packs made up or in Bulk, whatever in which any Goods, Wares, or Merchandizes are suspected to be packed or concealed."[16] Within the next five years, all seven of Paxton's fellow customs officers obtained similar writs.

During the French and Indian war, the use of writs of assistance quickly became routine. In August 1760, William Pitt the Elder, England's Southern Secretary of State (responsible for the American colonies), directed the then-Governor of Massachusetts Bay Colony, Sir Francis Bernard, to make further use of the instruments to prevent trade not just with French Canada, but with the French Indies as well.

Three months later, King George II died. According to British law, all writs of assistance expired within six months of a monarch leaving office. This gave the Crown only until April 1761 to renew them. An organization of merchants in the Massachusetts Bay Colony called "The Society for Promoting Trade and Commerce Within the Province" took the opportunity to petition the court to hear arguments against the Crown. The chief justice at the time was none other than Thomas Hutchinson—the man who had first brought the need to approach a court for a writ of assistance to Paxton's attention.

Boston's merchants chose James Otis Jr., one of the leading lawyers of the time, as their counsel. He had served as deputy advocate-general of the Massachusetts vice-admiralty court, but when the Crown solicited him to argue on its behalf, Otis refused and resigned his office. Instead, he agreed to represent the merchants pro bono. "The only principles of public conduct that are worthy of a gentleman, or a man," Otis later explained to the court, "are to sacrifice estate, ease, health, and applause, and even life, to the sacred calls of his country."[17]

Otis's oration challenging the writs of assistance became one of the most famous in U.S. history. More than half a century later, John Adams recalled, "Otis was a flame of fire!" His argument "breathed into this nation the breath of life." Adams continued, "Every man of an immense crowded audience appeared to me to go away as I did, ready to take arms against writs of assistance."[18]

The attack on general warrants lay at the heart of colonists' concept of liberty. It played a pivotal role in the founding of the country. As one 19th-century lexicographer, explained, "The issuing of [a writ of assistance] was one of the causes of the American republic."[19] Professor A. J. Langguth later observed, "James Otis stood up to speak, and something profound changed in America."[20]

What was it that Otis argued? He denounced the very concept of a general warrant: "I will to my dying day oppose, with all the powers and faculties God has given me, all such instruments of slavery on the one hand, and villainy on the other." General warrants exemplified "the worst instrument of arbitrary power, the most destructive of English liberty, and the fundamental principles of the constitution, that ever was found in an English law-book." Such power had "cost one King of England his head and another his throne."

Otis described the problem. Directed against all persons, "every one with this writ may be a tyrant"—and not just a tyrant, but one sanctioned by law. Being perpetual, no return was required. This meant that no one would ever be held accountable for its exercise. Anyone carrying the writ, moreover, could demand *others* to do his bidding, impacting their rights, and not just those of the individual being searched. "[O]ne of the most essential branches of English liberty," Otis further noted, "is the freedom of one's house. A man's house is his castle; and whilst he is quiet, he is as well guarded as a prince in his castle." A writ of assistance, "if it should be declared legal, would totally annihilate this privilege."

Otis warned about the potential misuse of writs for personal purposes. He cited a contemporary case in which a customs officer had employed a general warrant to exact revenge. "Every man," he argued, "prompted by revenge, ill humor or wantonness to inspect the inside of his neighbor's house, may get a writ of assistance; others will ask it from self defense; one arbitrary exertion will provoke another, until society will be involved in tumults and in blood."[21]

REJECTION OF GENERAL WARRANTS IN STATE CONSTITUTIONS

The founding generation went beyond merely objecting to general warrants. It established a positive right to be secure in one's person, home, papers, and effects, against unreasonable search and seizure. "Unreasonable" meant "contrary to reason," or, in the context of legal prose, contrary to the reason of the common law. General warrants, being contrary to common law, were illegal. The new American states therefore outlawed the use of general warrants as a concomitant of establishing the right against government intrusion.

The Founders insisted on specific warrants as the only legitimate instrument that could be used to invade the sanctity of one's home and papers. The states adopted a series of further, particular requirements that applied, without which even specific warrants would be considered invalid. These changes became anchored into American law in the nascent declarations of rights and state constitutions—well before the Fourth Amendment cemented them into the Constitution.

The fifth Virginia Convention took the first step along this path. In May 1776, a veritable Pantheon of the American Republic met to chart the future of the state. Patrick Henry, George Washington, Edmund Pendleton, George Mason, George Wythe, Richard Henry Lee, Thomas Jefferson, and others assembled in Williamsburg. Sitting in the House of Burgesses under the somber gaze of a portrait of George III, the delegates voted to draw up a declaration of rights, to draft a constitution establishing a new republic, and to form alliances with other colonies to create a new country. To George Mason fell the responsibility of writing the Virginia Declaration of Rights and, with James Madison, the Virginia Constitution. These documents became foundational for other state constitutions, the U.S. Constitution, and the Bill of Rights.

George Mason approached the declaration by underscoring the natural rights of man. Drawing heavily from political theories developed by Locke and Montesquieu, and building on English history and the British Constitution, while being cognizant of colonial experience, Mason committed to writing the idea that individuals hold certain rights, which limit what the government can do. The right to jury trial, freedom of the press, and freedom of religion all featured in his declaration, as did the right to be secure against "grievous and oppressive" search and seizure. To accomplish the last, Mason outlawed general warrants and laid down the particulars for what would be necessary for a specific warrant to issue.

The Virginia Declaration of Rights stated, "That general warrants, whereby an officer or messenger may be commanded to search suspected places without evidence of a fact committed, or to seize any person or persons not named, or whose offense is not particularly described and supported by evidence, are grievous and oppressive and ought not to be granted."[22] For a warrant to issue, evidence of a crime, the name of the person on whom the warrant would be served, and particularity with regard to the illegal activity for which the person was being sought or the search being conducted, would be required. On June 12, 1776, the fifth Virginia Convention adopted the declaration.

Pennsylvania was the next state to step forward. In July 1776, Benjamin Franklin, George Bryan, and James Cannon, along with the assistance of Thomas Paine and others, drafted the new state constitution. The document incorporated a declaration of rights as Article I. Adopted in September 1776, the Pennsylvania Constitution has come to be seen as one of the most democratic documents of the founding era—not least because of the universality of the vote and the structure of government that it instituted. The constitution included "security from searches and seizures" as a right guaranteed to the people. The relevant clause read, "The people shall be secure in their persons, houses, papers and possessions from unreasonable searches and seizures, and no warrant to search any place or to seize any person or things shall issue without describing them as nearly as may be, nor without probable cause, supported by oath or affirmation, subscribed to by the affiant."[23] By outlawing "unreasonable" search and seizure, Pennsylvania made general warrants illegal, even as it established additional particulars that would have to be met for specific warrants to be considered valid.

The Massachusetts Constitution, authored by John Adams, incorporated language strikingly similar to that adopted by Madison in the Bill of Rights. As such, it offers an important insight into the meaning of the Fourth Amendment.

Adams began by establishing a right: "Every subject has a right to be secure from all unreasonable searches and seizures of his person, his houses, his papers, and all his possessions."[24] The word "unreasonable" carried a particular meaning. It differed from our modern, relativistic sense of the word. The *Oxford English Dictionary*, for instance, currently defines "reasonable" as "Within the limits of what it would be rational or sensible to expect; not extravagant or excessive; moderate." "Unreasonable" means outside sensible limits, or "excessive in amount or degree."[25] In the 18th century, in contrast, "reasonable" meant consistent with the "reason of the Common Law," and "unreasonable" meant *against* the "reason of the Common Law"—that is, illegal.

The Massachusetts Constitution went on to refine what would be considered "unreasonable" in the context of a specific warrant: "All warrants, *therefore*, are contrary to this right, if the cause or foundation of them be not previously supported by oath or affirmation, and if the order in the warrant to a civil officer, to make search in suspected places, or to arrest one or more suspected persons, or to seize their property, be not accompanied with a special designation of the persons or objects of search, arrest, or seizure."[26]

By using "therefore" in this way, Adams clarified that it was to prevent a violation of the right against unreasonable search and seizure; that general warrants, and specific warrants lacking an oath, evidence, and particularity with regard to the persons to be arrested or places to be searched, would not be allowed. The document added an additional phrase, "and no warrant ought to be issued but in cases, and with the formalities, prescribed by the laws."[27] Only warrants that comported with the requirements would be valid.

The New Hampshire Constitution lifted the clauses used in the Massachusetts Constitution almost verbatim. Vermont, in turn, in the first chapter of its constitution, established a series of rights. Like the Massachusetts and New Hampshire clauses, Vermont began with a statement: "The people," it declared, "have a right to hold themselves, their houses, papers, and possessions, free from search or seizure." Security meant respect for the sanctity of one's home, person, papers, and possessions. Just as Adams had done in the case of the Massachusetts document, the Vermont Constitution followed this clause with "therefore," and then laid out a series of conditions that would have to be satisfied for a warrant to issue: it must be specific and limited, supported by oath or affirmation and sufficient evidence of a crime. Warrants lacking particularity violated the right. Delaware, Maryland, and North Carolina adopted a similar approach.[28]

The importance of these state declarations and constitutional documents cannot be overstated. They transformed a colonial grievance regarding overreach by the Crown into a written, constitutional guarantee of an individual right. They reflected the Founders' understanding of general warrants as the very definition of an unreasonable search and seizure, which violated the right of individuals to be secure. As such, general warrants were illegal. They demanded that, in order to protect the security of one's person, papers, and property against government overreach, warrants must contain sufficient particularity to prevent the abuse of power.

THE FOURTH AMENDMENT

In 1787 the constitutional convention met to address the deficiencies of the Articles of Confederation. The objective was to create a more powerful national government. But greater federal power generated apprehension that the new authorities could override the rights secured by state constitutions.

Accordingly, five days before the convention adjourned, George Mason expressed his wish that the Constitution be prefaced with a Bill of Rights. He offered to second any motion made for that purpose, as "It would give great quiet to the people."[29] Elbridge Gerry from Massachusetts supported Mason, but the effort failed. Upon transmission of the document to Congress, Richard Henry Lee, from Virginia, and Melancthon Smith, from New York, made another attempt. "Universal experience," Lee stated, had demonstrated the necessity of "the most express declarations and reservations . . . to protect the just rights and liberty of Mankind from the Silent, powerful, and ever active conspiracy of those who govern." The Constitution, therefore, should "be bottomed upon a declaration, or Bill of Rights, clearly and precisely stating the principles upon which the Social Compact is founded."[30] Among these was protection against "unreasonable" search and seizure of citizens' "papers, houses, persons, or property."[31] Congress declined the proposal and unanimously voted to forward the Constitution to the states, where the debate continued. Ratification hung in the balance.

Embedded in the argument about whether the Constitution needed a Bill of Rights was the importance of outlawing general warrants. One of the most sustained discussions arose in Virginia. Patrick Henry, the charismatic former governor, led the attack, declaring, "[O]ur rights and privileges are endangered, and the sovereignty of the states will be relinquished . . . all your immunities and franchises, all pretentions to human rights and privileges, are rendered insecure, if not lost by the new constitution." Writs of assistance held a special place of horror. "When these harpies are aided by excisemen, who may search, at any time, your houses, and most secret recesses," Henry asked, "will the people hear it? If you think so, you differ from me."

The Virginia Constitution prevented the state government "from issuing general warrants to search suspected places, or seize persons not named, without evidence of the commission of a fact, &c." But under the federal Constitution being contemplated, "The officers of congress may come upon you now, fortified with all the terrors of paramount federal authority." Henry warned, "Excisemen may come in multitudes; for the limitation of their numbers no man knows. They may, unless the general government be restrained by a bill of rights, or some similar restriction, go into your cellars and rooms, and search, ransack, and measure, every thing you eat, drink, and wear."[32] Any property could be taken "in the most arbitrary manner, without any evidence or reason." Everything considered sacred could "be searched and ransacked by the strong hand of power."[33]

Many in Virginia shared Henry's sentiments. As a result, the state convention appointed a committee to respond to the concerns. The proposed Bill of Rights, which the convention approved without any dissents (and which the committee had revised from the Virginia Declaration of Rights), was then transmitted, together with ratification of the Constitution, to Congress. It recommended, "That there be a declaration or bill of rights asserting, and securing from encroachment, the essential and unalienable rights of the people."[34]

As part of the proposed Bill of Rights, Virginia included language to establish the right against unreasonable search and seizure, tying protection of this right to the elimination of general warrants, as well as the inclusion of further elements that would be required for specific warrants to be valid.[35] Passage of a Bill of Rights was central to Virginia's ratification. Even with the accompanying statement of rights, the vote was close: delegates approved the Constitution by a vote of 89 to 79, giving supporters just a five-vote margin.

In New York, the vote was even closer. The final count was 30 to 27, giving approval only a two-vote margin. As in Virginia, the absence of provisions protecting individuals against promiscuous search figured largely in the public debate over ratification. A "Son of Liberty" predicted that general warrants would be one of the curses that would "be entailed on the people of America, by this preposterous and newfangled system, if they are ever so infatuated as to receive it." According to the writer, "Men of all ranks and conditions, subject to have their houses searched by officers, acting under the sanction of *general warrants*, their private papers seized, and themselves dragged to prison, under various pretenses, whenever the fear of their lordly masters shall suggest, that they are plotting mischief against their arbitrary conduct."[36]

New York delegates, accordingly, insisted on establishing the right against promiscuous search and seizure, including in its formal ratification the statement: "That every freeman has a right to be secure from all unreasonable searches and seizures of his person, his papers, or his property; and *therefore*, that all warrants to search suspected places, or seize any freeman, his papers, or property, without information, upon oath or affirmation, of sufficient cause, are grievous and oppressive; and that all general warrants (or such in which the place or person suspected are not particularly designated) are dangerous and ought not to be granted."[37] Two conditions would have to be met for an instrument not to be "unreasonable," or contrary to common law: general warrants would not be allowed; and specific warrants lacking information, oath, or sufficient cause, would not be issued. Instead, specific warrants would have to be based on sworn evidence of a specific crime committed and name the particular person on whom they would be served and place to be searched.

New York insisted that it was *only* with the understanding that Congress would amend the Constitution to take account of this right, and the others laid out in the document, that it consented to the new framework. The convention attached a military reservation to make it clear that it did not make its representation lightly: "[I]n full confidence, nevertheless, that, until a convention shall be called and convened for proposing amendments to the said Constitution, the militia of this state will not be continued in service out of this state for a longer term than six weeks, without the consent of the legislature thereof."[38] The threat underscored the seriousness with which the state viewed the protection of individual rights.

The U.S. Constitution would have been dead in the water had Virginia and New York refused to ratify it. The demand that general warrants be prohibited was not merely a sideshow to the founding. It was a central concern—one that persisted as the ratification debates were taken up state by state. Rhode Island drafted and forwarded a clause outlawing general warrants, as did Maryland. The latter condemned general warrants as "the great engine by which power may destroy those individuals who resist usurpation."[39] Accordingly, delegates considered inclusion of a clause prohibiting them to be indispensable. Massachusetts and North Carolina delegates similarly raised concern about the absence of any protections against promiscuous search and seizure, the latter drafting yet another clause outlawing the same, for inclusion in a Bill of Rights.

Pennsylvania held one of the liveliest discussions on the importance of banning general warrants. Samuel Bryan, an anti-Federalist writing as "Centinel," repeatedly made the point. "Your present frame of government," he warned, "secures you a right to hold yourselves, houses, papers and possessions free from search and seizure." Bryan continued, "therefore, warrants granted without oaths or affirmations first made, affording sufficient foundation for them . . . shall not be granted." The right hung in the balance: "whether your *papers*, your *persons*, and your *property*, are to be held sacred and free from *general warrants*, you are now to determine."[40] Other Anti-Federalists echoed Centinel's sentiments: "For the security of liberty," Brutus wrote, "it has been declared 'That all warrants, without oath or affirmation, to search suspected places, or seize any person, his papers or property, are grievous and oppressive.'" A provision banning such warrants was "as necessary under the general government as under that of the individual states."[41]

In June 1789, James Madison presented the U.S. House of Representatives with a draft of what is now the Fourth Amendment. The first clause—the right against unreasonable search and seizure—banned general warrants. The second clause went on to reject specific warrants that failed to meet the standard of "probable cause," were not "supported by oath or affirmation," or failed to describe "the places to be searched, or the persons or things to be seized." Madison proposed that the amendments be inserted into Article I(9). The only way in which the government could engage in general searches would be if Congress acquiesced, so it was the legislature that must be restrained.

The Committee of Eleven, chaired by John Vining from Delaware, made an important alteration. It changed Madison's language protecting persons, houses, papers, and *other property*, to persons, houses, papers, and *effects*. There are no records of why this change was made, but the shift is of some import. "Effects" carried a meaning beyond personal property or possessions to include commercial goods or items.[42] It was the equivalent of tangible goods.

Thereafter, only minor alterations occurred, outside of the location of the clause itself. Over Madison's objections, Roger Sherman moved for the relocation of the entire Bill of Rights into a separate appendix. He was concerned about how altering the main body of the document might affect the state ratification agreements, and he worried that inserting the clauses before the signatures of those present at Philadelphia would (mistakenly) suggest that they had also agreed to the amended text.

By leaving the word "place" in the singular and "persons or things" in the plural, the final clause reflected an understanding that considered multiple-specific search warrants, which confined a search to several places, to be invalid. Treatises written at the time repudiated the idea that multiple locations could be searched, restricting legitimate search to a specific location. As a result, warrants allowing numerous houses to be searched were considered unreasonable, even if the addresses were specified. By 1789, most states had introduced legislation requiring specific warrants, nearly all of which limited search warrants to single locations.

Soon after adoption of the Fourth Amendment, a series of cases reaffirmed that the purpose of the language was to protect individuals against the exercise of a general warrant or a specific warrant lacking evidence, probable cause, an oath, and particularity. By 1886, the Supreme Court had adopted an even broader concept of the realm covered by the Fourth Amendment, explicitly extending its protection of papers to include business records.[43]

GENERAL WARRANTS TODAY

There are some differences between the general warrants about which the Framers were concerned and those that mark the realm of foreign intelligence today. The founding generation did not live in a digital era. It was the invasion of the home that they sought to prevent. In contrast, the collection of digital information may not involve a physical trespass. Thus, it could be argued, it is not the sanctity of the home that is violated in digital monitoring, collection, and analysis, as no physical entry occurs. In the 18th century, in addition, the identity of those being searched was known. When the Crown entered a subject's home, it was clear who was under scrutiny. This was at the heart of concerns about public embarrassment.

In the contemporary context, in contrast, the collection programs are secret and indiscriminate. All people are subject to collection. Embarrassment is thus not (overtly) part of the equation.

Notwithstanding these distinctions, several of the recent FISC orders are strikingly similar to the general warrants that caused the Founders concern. It would be difficult to imagine a *better* example of a general warrant, than the *one* order, issued by FISC, authorizing the collection of international Internet and telephone content. It names approximately 90,000 targets, in the process monitoring millions of Americans' communications. The order is not premised upon prior suspicion of wrongdoing. It does not identify a particular place to be searched. The program is so massive that the government admits that it is impossible to state the number of citizens whose e-mails, telephone conversations, visual communications, and private documents are being monitored. Information obtained may be used to focus other surveillance authorities on individuals identified in the collection, as well as to bring criminal charges. It may be kept and shared with the military, with other agencies, and with foreign governments. The database constructed from this information may be queried using citizens' information, and it may be accessed for ordinary criminal prosecution, utterly unrelated to foreign intelligence collection.

PRISM and upstream collection are not the only efforts to obtain massive amounts of information under FISA. Starting in 2004, Internet metadata collection, and, in 2006, telephony metadata collection, similarly relied on judicial orders that lacked specificity. These orders did not specify or allege *any* crime prior to seizure. Nor was there oath or affirmation to support the same. They did not name any individual. They did not specify the place to be searched. They were used to *find* evidence of wrongdoing—without any prior offering of probable cause about a crime being committed. They carried a judicial imprimatur. And they involved compulsory process.

Companies served with the orders were forced to obey or face being held in contempt, just as individuals served with a writ of assistance at the time of the founding were forced to help the Crown to carry out the order.

The privacy interests implicated by these orders are consistent with those protected by the prohibition of general warrants. In the 18th century, the walls of one's home served as a proxy, within which citizens held dominion over their own affairs. Today, even if no physical entry may be entailed, the same type of information is being collected with deep implications for individuals' private lives. One's thoughts, one's beliefs, one's correspondence, and the nature and variety of one's relationships are all on the line. Since 1967, moreover, the courts have not premised Fourth Amendment protections solely on invasions of physical property. In response to new technologies, the Supreme Court found that it was the underlying privacy interest that mattered. In a digital world, individuals frequently take steps to secure their privacy, using passwords, signing contracts with companies that have privacy policies, and even using encryption to send their communications. The orders issued by FISC fail to acknowledge the equivalent of such shut doors, collecting private information en masse.

The Founders worried about the collection of private information. It was at the point of seizure that the prohibition on promiscuous search *and seizure* kicked in. For the government to now assume that it can collect all this data, with no prior specificity, on the grounds that it will examine only a small portion of the records rather begs the point. As in the 18th century, the potential for abuse of the aggrandizement of all this information in one place is substantial. If anything, the argument against the collection of this information is even stronger in light of the digitization of so much personal information and the potential application of sophisticated algorithms to this data, in the process generating more knowledge about citizens' private lives.

It could be argued that fidelity to the original meaning of the Constitution, or the language introduced by the Founders, is of little consequence. The essence of the text, one could reason, does and ought to change over time. But in the context of the rapid expansion in surveillance authorities, there are two problems with this assertion. First, as the next chapter suggests, it fails to appreciate the strength of the arguments that persuaded the Founders to reject promiscuous search and seizure—reasons that continue to be salient today. Second, as addressed in Chapter 6, living constitutionalism does allow for the application of new rules of construction. But however incremental such changes might be, surely they cannot mean that the protections created at the founding cease to exist—or, even more preposterously—that the language of the Fourth Amendment means the *opposite* of what it meant when it was enacted.

CHAPTER FIVE

...

General Warrants

WHY DID GENERAL warrants earn the enmity of the founding generation?[1] Was it merely the context of the times or an accident of history that these instruments fell from use? Or are the arguments offered by legal scholars, such as Coke, Hale, and Blackstone; the objections raised by Otis's fiery oration; and the rationales that drove state measures banning general warrants and then the incorporation of these measures into the Fourth Amendment still relevant today?

Certainly, the Framers were concerned about national security. If anything, there was even more urgency in 1787 than now. The Union itself hung in the balance. Yet the Founders did *not* provide the federal government with the authority to introduce general warrants for the common defense. Like their English predecessors, they *rejected* reason of state as a sufficiently grave threat to waive the prohibition. Nor was the government allowed to intrude upon the private sphere, absent sufficient cause and particularity. There were no exceptions for libel, treason, or other crimes. Close inspection of why this was the case underscores the extent to which the principles that undergirded the adoption of the Fourth Amendment transcend time. The potential impact on individual rights, the risk of concrete harms that accompanied giving the government access to citizens' private lives, and the dangers inherent in a structural imbalance of power remain important concerns.

RIGHTS

The most common argument offered at the Founding against promiscuous search and seizure centered on the violation of fundamental rights. General warrants were not the only way in which citizens' liberty could be violated, but the founding generation considered them amongst the most egregious.

The interest stemmed from the right to be secure in one's own abode against unwelcome intrusion. Anti-Federalist writings repeatedly emphasized that an Englishman's home was his castle. The walls served to protect individuals from the outside world. Embedded in this concept were deeper assumptions about what one ought—and ought not—to be forced to make available to others or to the government. Access to one's home suggested access to one's family and friends, bedroom and closets, diaries and even pockets. One's most intimate secrets would be exposed. Writing in 1764 as the Father of Candor, John Almon argued that no gentleman "would rest easy in his bed, if he thought, that . . . he was liable not only to be taken up himself, but every secret of his family made subject to the inspection of a whole Secretary of State's office." He continued, "Many gentlemen have secret correspondences, which they keep from their wives, their relations, and their bosom friends. Every body has some private papers, that he would not on any account have revealed." Giving the government such authority would be "inconsistent with every idea of liberty."

Solitude also mattered. Protecting the home allowed individuals a safe haven, within which they could retreat from the world outside. As the world has become more complex, the importance of creating a sphere within which others could not intrude has grown. By the end of the 19th century, Samuel Warren and Louis Brandeis keyed into this as one of the most important aspects of life. They explained, "The intensity and complexity of life, attendant upon advancing civilization, have rendered necessary some retreat from the world." They thus took it upon themselves "to consider whether the existing law affords a principle which can properly be invoked to protect the privacy of the individual," and, if so, what "the nature and extent of such protection" might be.[2]

The importance of creating a sanctuary has, if anything, become stronger in the intervening years, as social networks have become increasingly complex, technology more advanced, and the pace of life swifter. There is a value to establishing a sphere into which others may reach only under limited conditions.

The creation of private space makes it possible to develop autonomy, ideas, and self. It allows us to question the world and to grow, to learn and to evolve. It is a personal right in that it relates directly to individual health and well-being. It gives us the opportunity to relax, to be unguarded in our actions and ideas, and to question the world and our role in it. The evolution of self requires the ability to have such a protected space, allowing us to interact with our own thoughts, ideas, and beliefs. In this way, it is essential to self-determination.

Scholars through the ages have written about the intrinsic value of a division between public life and the private sphere. Perhaps the most famous is Aristotle's distinction between the realm of political activity (πολlις) and private family life (οικοs). J. S. Mill built on this distinction in *On Liberty*, arguing that while government most properly controls the former, the self dictates the latter. Protecting private affairs from the state allows individuals to evolve.

Underlying this approach is a critical insight: exposing one's private life to others' eyes affects behavior. If we feel that what we say and do, in private, will be seen, or recorded and analyzed, by others, then we moderate our actions. There is a basic, Kantian view here that the ability to pursue our own values, without others limiting our thoughts, actions, and perceptions, is central to our ability to define ourselves. It matters for our personal and moral development. It is essential to our intellectual development. And it is critical for our political engagement.

Liberal, democratic states are premised on the understanding that voters are rational beings with access to ideas. To make informed decisions, it must be possible to think, to question, and to debate the appropriate course of action. The health of the political community depends upon it. The right to privacy, in this sense, is linked to other rights, such as free speech and free association—values that allow for the exchange of ideas and, through such exchanges, the evolution of knowledge, understanding, and views.

These ideas were very much alive in colonial America. William Penn was subject to a general warrant and wrote forcefully against them. In his *Frame of Government*, he went beyond objecting to promiscuous searches to laying out the conditions for optimal personal and political development. He emphasized freedom of conscience and freedom of speech as essential for the open exchange of ideas. The same flexibility that must be reflected in the structure of the political community had to mark individual thought. The best way to accomplish this, for Penn, was to develop one's own ideas and then to allow for open exchange. Spiritual vitality required the establishment of a realm for personal intellectual and moral growth. The entrusting of such ideas to others allowed for their evolution.

Linked to this instrumental concept is the idea that control over private information allows individuals to determine who one is in the wider world. Even as it helps to develop personality and self, giving an individual control over what to reveal to others gives us the option of whom we will be—to others. We do not have to be defined by what we say and do in private. There is thus an element of choice involved.

To the extent that private information is obtained, recorded, and analyzed, it leads to a cementing of self and a narrowing of options. By crossing into public space, information may limit who we can be in the outside world. It constrains choice. Privacy stems in part from being able to regulate what others know about us, the extent to which they can access us, and to what degree we become the subject of others' attention.

Another concept embedded in the idea of an Englishman's home as his castle was the liberty to decide, for oneself, whom one includes in one's intimate affairs and the extent to which those with whom one is connected are brought in to one's personal sphere. Unlike individual liberty or the humanistic concept of self-development, this is a social right in that it relates to relationships between individuals. Intimacy deepens relationships. Giving individuals control over their own sphere provides them with the freedom to determine with whom they choose to share their intimate lives. This is part of what it means to be human—to connect to others around us.

Government intrusion in this sphere may have far-reaching effects. Intimacy develops important aspects of self. Social relationships premised on love, friendship, and respect contribute benefits that range from personal development to a sense of security and belonging. The integrity of these relationships is a social good. It matters for the well-being of individual members of society, as well as for the construction of connectedness between people, which, in turn, creates a stronger social fabric.

By selecting with whom one shares the intimate details of one's life, it is possible to maintain different types of relationships. Such diversity also carries value. The reasons one may want to develop relationships may vary. It may be for financial security, for protection, for learning, or for creativity. It may be to start a family or to experience spiritual growth. Exposing these relationships to outside eyes may change the nature of the relationship or limit the range of relationships in which one engages. Individuals subject to surveillance may change their behavior in ways that hurt social interaction and the ability of individuals to build strong relationships.

Beyond the privacy rights discussed thus far (individual liberty, freedom from intrusion, and intimacy), general warrants threaten associated rights. As the Supreme Court has repeatedly recognized, due process is imperiled by the broad collection of information on citizens. Fear of associational biases may prevent individuals from forming friendships with others who follow a different religious doctrine. The concern may be either that that relationship will be placed under scrutiny, or that, because of the relationship, other areas of one's life will be placed under scrutiny. Intimacy, education, and spiritual growth suffer. It makes little sense to speak of free speech if general warrants can collect everything an individual says and then analyze that information for patterns.

It is not just the rights of the target at stake but the rights of others who are associated with the target. In the 18th century, Almon protested that government clerks would peruse private letters "of the gentleman himself, and of all his friends and acquaintances of both sexes." Wilkes's patron, Lord Grenville-Temple, similarly noted that the momentum of disclosure went beyond the individual whose papers were seized, to all those with whom the person was in correspondence. Liberty of the person, liberty from intrusion, intimacy and social relationships, and the associated rights of due process, free association, and free speech are all affected for individuals whose information is implicated in promiscuous searches.

In the Section 702 program, PRISM collection is based on selectors submitted to U.S.-based service providers, giving them access to stored communications, real-time collection, and Voice over Internet

Protocol (VoIP). Everyone linked to the selector has his or her stored communications, real-time conversations, and voice interactions collected. For upstream collection, the net is cast wider. It is not just communications directly linked to the "selector" but anything "about" the selector that is obtained—anywhere in the world. The number of people affected is impossible to calculate—a fact the Director of National Intelligence has consistently argued in response to questions meant to elicit a number of precisely how many Americans have had their privacy infringed by programmatic collection.

In the Section 215 program, significant numbers of people were similarly affected. For years, the government ran the telephony metadata collection program out to three "hops." The math matters. Suppose that an individual is in contact with 50 people. The second "hop" out brings the government into contact with 2,500 people. The third "hop" increases the number of people affected to more than 100,000. But even these calculations are low. They do not take into account high-volume numbers dialed, such as restaurants or delivery services, or widely shared telephone numbers, such as customer service lines or VoIP protocol bridges.[3] The latter category, in particular, may quickly implicate millions of people in just one "hop."

Social network metadata may be even more encompassing. Suppose that an individual has 50 "friends" on Facebook. The company states that the average user has 190 "friends," 14 percent of who are "friends" with each other. With these numbers in mind, the next "hop" out brings the government into contact with 8,170 people. The third "hop" increases the number of people affected to more than 1.3 million—more than the entire population of Maine.[4]

Setting aside for the moment the impact of collecting metadata at the front end, the ability to initiate secondary or tertiary surveillance two or three hops out, on suspicious numbers or accounts because they are in contact with people who are in contact with the target (or one further step removed), quickly implicates thousands, if not millions, of people. The same could be true of Internet metadata, e-mail metadata, and other forms of communications.

For each person implicated in such analyses, the right to privacy and other, associated rights have now been compromised. For tight-knit communities, or those targeted because of political, religious, or other views, the impact is likely to be disproportionately felt by one section of society, raising further concerns about the impact on minorities and the broader ability of society to mediate social, political, and religious differences.

HARMS

Another set of arguments that circulated at the Founding against promiscuous search and seizure focused on the concrete harms that could follow from allowing the government to have access to citizens' private lives. James Otis and others emphasized that the approach to obtaining information was the wrong way around: instead of having evidence that indicated an individual was engaged in criminal activity, and basing a breach of the rights at stake on the information, general warrants suspended rights in order to uncover incriminating information. This approach undermined the concept of innocent until proven guilty. Instead, it assumed the potential guilt of all citizens, whose innocence could only be demonstrated following a search.

The chief concern was that the inversion created an opportunity for the government to target individuals without evidence of criminal activity—a power easily abused. It could be directed against individuals or ethnic groups, political organizations, or religious entities. The government could use a general warrant to gain insight into citizens' lives and social relationships and then employ the information obtained to prevent opposition, to stifle opposing views, or to disrupt organizations.

New technologies magnify the potential for harm. Information obtained under Section 702 might signal illegal activity. But such data represents a minute portion of what is actually obtained. An even smaller fraction may relate to foreign intelligence. Most data will neither relate to nor indicate criminal behavior. But its collection will make us extremely vulnerable.

In 1721, William Hawkins wrote in *Pleas of the Crown* that promiscuous search and seizure may prove "highly prejudicial to the reputation as well as the liberty of the party." In 1765, Westminster returned to this danger. In the 19th century, scholars noted that, "even when conducted in the discreetest [sic.] manner," general warrants "might injure the most virtuous in their reputation and fortune." Although a general warrant may not create an explicit right to seize an innocent individual, it could nevertheless "throw in the way of messengers a temptation to inquire into the life and character of persons."[5]

Access to the innermost details of individuals' lives creates the possibility that private information can be used as leverage. Data can be used to cast aspersions on people with a deleterious impact on their reputation and standing, quite apart from any civil or criminal penalties that may result. Blackmail is not a pleasant concept. Yet it is a real phenomenon that has, in the past, been used by the executive branch against its adversaries. It would be short-sighted to assume that it could not happen in the future.

The type of information currently being obtained under FISA could be used to consolidate control or to prevent political, social, economic, or other challenge to the ruling élite. The concentration of power is disturbing in a democratic state—particularly when secretly conducted, outside of the public gaze. The temptation to use it to head off opposition may be too great to overcome. History is replete with examples. Watergate, perhaps, is one of the most famous. But even more recent examples, of much less onerous authorities, illustrate the point.

Consider tax breaks. Beginning in 2010, the Internal Revenue Service (IRS) initiated a more aggressive review procedure of applicants for tax-exempt status, directing offices across the country to "Be on the Look Out" for entities using certain terms, such as "Tea Party," "Patriots," or "9/12 Project." The IRS targeted organizations whose issues included government spending, government debt, or taxes; those that sought to educate the public by advocacy or lobbying to make America a better place to live; and those whose files included any statements criticizing how the country was being run.

The U.S. Department of Treasury followed the scandal that erupted with the self-flagellating report, *Inappropriate Criteria Were Used to Identify Tax-Exempt Applications for Review*. It found that in addition to using political criteria as a trigger for greater scrutiny, the IRS routinely forwarded inappropriate questions to targeted organizations. Queries included the names of donors; a list of issues important to the organization (and the organization's position on the issues); whether the director planned to run for public office; the political affiliation of the officer, director, speakers, and any candidates the organization supported; information regarding directors' employment outside the organization; and information on other groups that the IRS suspected the organization could provide. In May 2013 the IRS publicly apologized for inappropriately targeting conservative groups.

The Obama administration was not the first to misuse the agency's power. Almost every administration since the inception of the IRS has used the organization for political purposes.[6] President Franklin Roosevelt turned the IRS's resources against newspapers opposed to the New Deal, as well as political rivals. President John F. Kennedy launched an Ideological Organizations Audit Project, which focused on right-leaning political organizations, such as the American Enterprise Institute and the Foundation for Economic Education. A Senate committee concluded that organizations had been selected "because of their political activity and not because of any information that they had violated the tax laws."[7] President Richard Nixon created a Special Services Staff, which marshaled "all IRS activities involving ideological, military, subversive, radical, and similar type organizations."[8]

General warrants for the collection of communications and other digital data create a similar potential for mischief but on a much broader scale and with some of the most coercive powers of the state—those related to criminal law and national security—attached. History here proves instructive. The same pattern—leveraging the power of the government to obtain information to undermine political opposition—marks the realm of national security generally, and the NSA in particular.

In the late 1960s the NSA built a watch list that rapidly expanded. Project MINARET began by focusing on citizens traveling to Cuba, but it quickly branched out to include civil rights leaders, people suspected of criminal activity, and drug users. Operation Shamrock, in turn, allowed the NSA to obtain copies of international telegrams that had originated in, or been forwarded through, the United States. It expanded from focusing on foreign targets to incorporating citizens' communications.

The lesson of history is that even where efforts are made to *restrict* programs to the most serious threats to the country, over time they expand. The tool becomes a useful way to pursue other interests. The result is a form of intelligence creep in which more and more use is made of the data.

The programs conducted under FISA's amended provisions overshadow those that gave birth to the statute in the first place. The new authorities are already being used for criminal law purposes unrelated to foreign intelligence. As the Privacy and Civil Liberties Oversight Board noted, the FBI does not even bother to log the number of times it queries the Section 702 database. The commingling of data and its dissemination to other agencies underscores the concern that this information may be used in unanticipated ways.

Some potential uses of foreign intelligence information may have nothing to do with criminal law. At the same time, they may reflect compelling state interests, which generate demand for obtaining information in ways that further erode citizens' rights.

For example, what if the government wanted to use Section 702 to find out if anyone entering the country had been infected with a deadly virus? Recent outbreaks underscore the dangers posed by infectious disease. In February 2015, the Department of State issued a travel alert to citizens planning to travel to Sierra Leone, noting that an outbreak of Ebola had spurred the Centers for Disease Control and Prevention to issue a Level 3 Travel Warning. The Bureau of Consular Affairs recommended that Americans undertake only essential travel to the region. While the Department of Homeland Security introduced enhanced screening procedures at five U.S. airports for individuals entering from Sierra Leone, travelers could still pass through screening prior to becoming symptomatic.

According to the World Health Organization, Ebola has a fatality rate that varies from 25 percent to 90 percent.[9] It would be logical for the government to use any instruments at its disposal to try to ensure greater health protections—particularly for a disease as devastating as hemorrhagic fever. One could even make a colorable national security argument for the use of 702 data in this manner, as public health is vital to the economy, and to citizens' lives. Should the government be allowed to use foreign intelligence information for public health purposes?

The temptation to use such information to protect life may be too great to overcome. Whatever protections are built into the back end, as time progresses, little by little, the information will be used. It will be used for criminal law. It will be used for public health. It will be used for myriad other purposes, far afield from the purpose for which it was collected. And the aggrandizement of so much power, in one place, will be subject to abuse.

The Founders objected to the consolidation of power. They looked to Chief Justice Charles Pratt's recognition in *Leach v. Money* that such a power could "be productive of great oppression."[10] As Pratt echoed in *Wilkes v. Wood*, "a discretionary power given to [officers] to search wherever their suspicions may chance to fall . . . is totally subversive to the liberty of the subject."[11] In his oration in *Paxton's Case*, James Otis expressed a similar concern, recounting a recent incident, in which a customs officer had attempted to use writs of assistance to exact revenge on a constable. John Dickinson's *Letters of a Pennsylvania Farmer* decried writs of assistance as being open to abuse, as did the anti-Federalists, convinced of the dangers at hand.

Debates over the states' declarations of rights and constitutions, and the state constitutional conventions, routinely recognized the danger of giving this power to the government. Patrick Henry shuddered at the arbitrary manner in which men's papers could be searched and possessions seized. In Connecticut, one of the first courts to consider general warrants after the adoption of the Bill of Rights observed that general warrants "would open a door for the gratification of the most malignant passions, if such process issued by a magistrate should screen him from damages."[12]

If anything, the problem is even more profound today. Bulk and programmatic collection create the potential for social and political control on a scale the Founders could not have even imagined.

DISTRIBUTION OF POWER

Another set of concerns that marked the public debate over the illegality of general warrants related to the distribution of power. It was not just too much power to the government-writ-large, but too much power to the executive branch, without adequate constraints from the other branches. General warrants amounted to the fox guarding the hen house. Put in more learned words, *nemo iudex in causa sua*: no one should be a judge in his own cause. This phrase reflects one of the central tenets of common law and the understanding that anyone with an interest at stake risks partiality in their judgment. It is fundamental to the concept of fairness.

It was no less than Lord Coke, in *Dr. Bonham's Case*, who famously held that a college of physicians provided with statutory authority to punish individuals who practiced medicine without a license could not simultaneously act as "judges, ministers, and parties."[13] In his *Pleas of the Crown*, William Hawkins criticized promiscuous search as it gave the officer the discretion of determining whom and where to search. Lord Mansfield similarly noted in *Leach v. Money* that general warrants were illegal under common law because an officer should not have the discretion to determine the extent of his own power.

The American colonists embraced the English legal arguments. In Pennsylvania and Virginia, judges used similar reasoning against the writs authorized by the Townshend Act of 1767, noting that officers should not be given such power.[14] It is a principle intimately connected with the Fourth Amendment. As one scholar explained to the Massachusetts Historical Society as he read the text of the Fourth Amendment, "No public officer, therefore, in this country, can be supplied with a general warrant for use on occasion, he to be the judge of the occasion. About that there can hardly be a question."[15]

Underlying this principle is a simple fact. The executive branch is not a disinterested observer where its own interests are at stake. By giving it a free pass to determine the extent of its authority, the risk of aggrandizement of power is substantial. General warrants leave it to the executive to determine whom to target, where to look, and what to collect. Not only could this lead to ever-greater power, but also the executive could use it against the other branches. It could target those opposed to its policies by placing members of Congress and their staffs, or members of the judiciary and others associated with the functioning of the courts, under surveillance. The impact on the division of federal authority is hard to ignore. One need not look far to find ready examples.

In 2002, the CIA began a secret rendition, detention, and interrogation program. The agency neglected to brief members of the Senate Select Committee on Intelligence (SSCI) until September 2006. Just over a year later, *The New York Times* reported that the CIA had destroyed videotapes of its enhanced interrogations. SSCI requested a briefing from Director Michael Hayden, who assured the committee that detailed written records existed. The chair of the Senate committee sent staff members to the CIA to review the documents. The initial report suggested that the interrogation techniques used went beyond those that the CIA had admitted to Congress. In March 2009, the committee voted to conduct a comprehensive review of the program.

Over the next three years, as the Senate staff pored over millions of cables, e-mails, memos, and other documents, the politics became increasingly heated. The Senate was to be provided with a separate, offsite computer system segregated from the CIA's network. Only the agency's technology personnel would have access to the system, except as otherwise authorized by the Senate committee.[16]

As it became increasingly apparent that SSCI was going to issue a report sharply critical of the CIA, the agency placed SSCI's computers under surveillance. The CIA's acting general counsel accused SSCI staffers of criminal actions, referring the case to DOJ for prosecution.

When the information became public in 2014, Senator Diane Feinstein expressed "grave concerns that the CIA's [actions] may well have violated the separation of powers principles embodied in the United States Constitution." She worried that it "undermined the constitutional framework essential to effective congressional oversight of intelligence activities or any other government function."[17]

The CIA inspector general launched an investigation into the matter. In July 2014 he released a summary of his report, verifying that CIA employees had, indeed, inappropriately accessed SSCI computers and e-mail accounts, and determining that the criminal charges had been based on false claims. Six months later, the CIA announced that the inspector general was leaving the agency to "pursue an opportunity in the private sector."[18]

In light of the mounting tension over the results of the SSCI report into the CIA's interrogation programs, the agency's actions look very much like the executive branch using surveillance to try to head off political opposition from another branch of government. The incident underscores the risk that surveillance may be employed to undermine structures built to constrain power. Even where Congress approves the contours of a program, its inability to examine every use of the data creates a shield for the executive to use information in ways that override structural protections.

Like the legislature, the judicial branch may be a target of surveillance efforts. To the extent that all individuals' communications are being intercepted, this information can then be used to advantage the executive—again raising separation of powers concerns.

This issue was at the heart of a challenge to the Section 702 program. Section 4 of the minimization procedures address attorney-client communications. "As soon as it becomes apparent that a communication is between a person who is known to be under criminal indictment in the United States and an attorney who represents that individual in the matter under indictment," the document states, "monitoring of that communication will cease and the communication will be identified as an attorney-client communication in a log maintained for that purpose."[19] At that point, DOJ's National Security Division must be notified so that appropriate procedures may be undertaken "to protect such communications from review or use in any criminal prosecution, while preserving foreign intelligence information."[20]

The rationale behind limiting attorney-client privilege in the national security context only to those who have been indicted (and individuals representing them) is that the Sixth Amendment right to counsel applies after indictment. However, as a matter of ordinary civil or criminal law, an individual may have privileged communications with an attorney prior to that point.

In other words, under the Section 702 program, the government can collect, analyze, and use the information in ways that may be prejudicial to the conduct of a trial. There is evidence that this is precisely what is being done.

Perhaps the most well-known case is that of the Islamic charity al-Haramain Foundation, which was under investigation for providing material support to a terrorist organization. In August 2004 the government mistakenly provided defense lawyers with a log of the telephone calls between them and their clients. As soon as the FBI realized the mistake, it demanded that the lawyers return the documents. In another situation, in 2009, an individual suspected of terrorist activity, Adis Medunjanin, tried to call an attorney. Over the next 6 months, they spoke 42 times. Following Medunjanin's arrest for attempting to bomb the New York subway, his lawyer found a CD with recordings of all of his conversations with his client in the classified files. Such information, in criminal law, would be privileged. But in the context of national security, it was part and parcel of developing the case against Medunjanin, as well as part of the prosecution.

Other allegations regarding the impact of intelligence collection on the conduct of trials have been made. The proceedings in

Guantánamo Bay have been stalked by defense teams' concerns that the intelligence agencies have deployed various forms of surveillance to gain the upper hand. In April 2013, in the wake of charges of secret government monitoring of defense communications, the *Washington Post* reported that hundreds of thousands of defense e-mails had been turned over to the prosecution.[21] The breach spurred the chief military defense counsel to order all attorneys to stop using Defense Department networks to transmit privileged communications. In April 2014, the FBI approached a member of a defense team at his home and asked him to sign a document that suggested he might be asked to provide the FBI with information on an ongoing basis in the future. In February 2013, the *Washington Post* reported that microphones were hidden inside devices that, outwardly, look like smoke detectors, in the rooms in which attorneys meet detainees.

The protection of attorney-client privilege is considered one of the oldest principles of the law, on the grounds that attorneys cannot adequately provide representation if the communications are being monitored. There is an exception where the lawyers themselves are suspected of criminal or fraudulent activity. But in the cases that have emerged, the lawyers are not suspected of anything. In criminal law, all privileged calls, whether prior to or following indictment, must be minimized and destroyed. Not so in the realm of national security—despite the use of the criminal justice system for prosecution.

This issue has generated such concern among those in the legal profession that in February 2014 the president of the American Bar Association, James Silkenat, wrote on behalf of the organization's nearly 400,000 members to NSA Director General Keith B. Alexander and General Counsel Rajesh De, to express concern about the potential harm to what he referred to as "a bedrock legal principle of our free society," critical in both the civil and criminal contexts. He noted that the privilege is essential to the fundamental right to effective counsel. It "encourages clients to seek out and obtain guidance to conform their conduct to the law, facilitates self-investigation into past conduct to identify shortcomings and remedy problems, and enables lawyers to fulfill their ethical duties to their clients, all of which benefit society at large."[22] General Alexander responded that the NSA was "firmly committed to the rule of law and the bedrock legal principle of attorney-client privilege."[23] He considered the minimization procedures sufficient.

The purpose behind separation of powers is to prevent the accumulation of too much power in one place. The risk is that surveillance will override these structural protections. Under the FISA programs, legislators' and judges' personal communications can be monitored by the executive branch, without any prior suspicion of wrongdoing. Linked to this argument is a broader institutional one: namely, the expansion of powers granted to the executive results in a diminution of authority to the judiciary. In his *Commentaries on the Laws of England*, Blackstone explained: "[I]t is the duty of the magistrate, and ought not be left to the officer, to judge the grounds of suspicion."[24] Patrick Henry suggested that the insertion of the judiciary ensured that evidence and reason mitigated the "strong hand of power."[25] Removing judges from these determinations invites abuse and threatens the rule of law.

CHAPTER SIX

...

What Is an "Unreasonable" Search?

ONE POSSIBLE RESPONSE to the argument that bulk collection violates the Constitution, or that it belies its basic principles and values, is that the kind of information being collected is not protected by the Fourth Amendment. This approach emanates from a line of cases referred to as "third-party doctrine." The central idea, which the Supreme Court articulated in the 1970s, is that third-party information—like telephony metadata held by Verizon—is not private. By placing a call, customers voluntarily give information to the telephone company, such as whom one is telephoning; how long one talks; and what numbers, in return, are calling the customer. The data allows businesses to provide services and to bill their customers accordingly.

This approach, applied in the contemporary context, extends the province of third-party information to all customer records. Without trunk identifier information, a company cannot guarantee that mobile telephones receive or send calls. If companies fail to provide Internet access, consumers cannot use SnapChat, Vine, or

Instagram. The amount of information conveyed from the customer's use of an iPhone or Android device to the telephone company is not the issue. It is the *quality* of the information that matters. So if certain information is not protected, then *more* of the same information similarly would not be protected. Zero plus zero equals, well, zero. Ergo, collection of this information is not a search within the meaning of the Fourth Amendment.

Those who make this argument point to *Smith v. Maryland* and *United States v. Miller*, two cases that shaped the evolution of third-party doctrine. They stand for the proposition that "[T]he Fourth Amendment does not prohibit the obtaining of information revealed to a third party and conveyed by him to Government authorities, even if the information is revealed on the assumption that it will be used only for a limited purpose and the confidence placed in the third party will not be betrayed."[1]

As existing doctrine goes, this is a solid legal argument. The Supreme Court has not directly overturned these cases, one of which explicitly turned on whether individuals have a privacy interest in the numbers dialed from their telephone.

The problem is that these cases are four decades old. They no longer reflect how the world works or the privacy interests of the digital age. The type of information that companies now have about customers departs from that available in the mid-1970s. It is not just more of the same information that is being collected—but new information—with unique implications for privacy. *Smith* did not consider whether police officers could compel a company to turn over all of its customers' metadata to build a detailed picture of formal and informal social networks, which could then be analyzed to look for potentially illegal activity. The information being sought is not different in degree. It is different in kind. So it is not zero plus zero. It is zero plus one yottabyte—which is a lot of information and a much deeper incursion into privacy than just the dialing information from a landline in 1976.

SMITH V. MARYLAND

On March 5, 1976, Patricia McDonough was walking down the street in Baltimore, when a man grabbed her purse and ran. She reported the crime, providing the police with a description of the man who assaulted her, as well as a 1975 Monte Carlo car she had seen near the scene. Soon afterward, McDonough started receiving threatening and obscene phone calls at home from a man who identified himself as the thief. At one point, the caller told her to go out on her front porch. When she did so, the Monte Carlo drove slowly past her home.

The cops observed a car of the same description in her neighborhood. Tracing the license plate, they discovered that the car was registered to Michael Lee Smith. The next day, the police asked the telephone company to install a pen register to trace the numbers called from Smith's home telephone. The company agreed. That day Smith called McDonough's home. The police then applied for, and obtained, a search warrant. They executed the warrant and, upon entering Smith's house, found a telephone book with the corner turned down to McDonough's name and number. In a subsequent six-man lineup, McDonough identified Smith as the person who had robbed her.

Confronted with these facts, the Supreme Court determined that Michael Lee Smith did not have a reasonable expectation of privacy in the numbers dialed from his telephone. The key sentence from the decision centered on the customer's relationship with the telephone company: "A person has no legitimate expectation of privacy in information he voluntarily turns over to third parties."[2] This line contributed to the evolution of third-party doctrine. Information voluntarily provided to others, such as telecommunication companies or Internet service providers, divests individuals of any right to Fourth Amendment protections.

Smith v. Maryland echoed another case from the 1970s that sought to clarify the limits of the "reasonable expectation of privacy" test established by *Katz*. Recall that in 1967, the court had replaced the requirement of a physical intrusion with an approach centered on the objective and subjective reading of what one would consider private. It was not clear how this principle would apply across the board.

In 1973, prosecutors charged bootlegger Mitch Miller of failing to pay liquor tax on alcohol distilling equipment and whiskey. As part of their investigation, the Bureau of Alcohol, Tobacco, and Firearms subpoenaed Miller's bank records. The Court of Appeals for the Fifth Circuit determined that Miller's privacy interest in his financial records had been violated, in contravention of the Fourth Amendment. The Supreme Court disagreed. In a 6-3 opinion, it held that the documents were not Miller's private papers but rather part of each bank's business records. Neither owning nor possessing the documents, Miller lacked an expectation of privacy in them.[3]

In its application to FISC for the telephony metadata program, the government heavily relied on these precedents, and *Smith* in particular, to argue that it was constitutional. In its August 2013 White Paper defending the program, the Department of Justice stated that a Section 215 order is not a search because "as the Supreme Court has expressly held participants in telephone calls lack any reasonable expectation of privacy under the Fourth Amendment in the telephone numbers dialed."[4] In *ACLU v. Clapper*, the government cited the Court's reasoning in *Smith* to assert that, even if a subscriber harbored a subjective expectation that the numbers dialed would remain private, it would not be reasonable because individuals have "no legitimate expectation of privacy in information" voluntarily turned over to third parties.[5] Because courts have followed *Smith* to find no reasonable expectation of privacy in the sending or receipt of e-mail and Internet protocol addressing information, as well as subscriber information, "*Smith* is fatal to Plaintiffs' claim that the collection of metadata records of their communications violates the Fourth Amendment."[6]

FISC accepted the government's position. Judge Claire V. Eagan relied almost exclusively on *Smith* in her August 2013 opinion, dispensing of any possible constitutional claim in a matter of a few paragraphs. "The production of telephone service provider metadata is squarely controlled by the U.S. Supreme Court decision in *Smith v. Maryland*."[7] She reasoned that because customers are aware that telephone service providers maintain call detail records in the normal course of business, they assume the risk that the telephone company will provide those records to the government. That information was collected in bulk was of no consequence: "[W]here one individual does not have a Fourth Amendment interest, grouping together a large number of similarly-situated individuals cannot result in a Fourth Amendment interest springing into existence *ex nihilo*."[8]

These analyses turn a blind eye to the ways in which the privacy interests impacted by the use of pen/trap devices and their application to broad sectors of the population have changed as technology has advanced and new analytical tools have come into being. The interests that the Court confronted in the 1970s are different than those that characterize third-party information today.

To be clear: the Court's decision in *Smith* was based solely on whether the numbers dialed were protected or not. Once this information was obtained and combined with the facts of the case, the police used it to obtain a search warrant. But context is everything.

In *Smith*, the police did not obtain a warrant prior to installing the pen register, but they clearly had reasonable suspicion that the target of the surveillance, Michael Lee Smith, had robbed, threatened, intimidated, and harassed Patricia McDonough. The police installed the pen register consistent with their suspicion that Smith was engaged in criminal wrongdoing.

Under Section 215, in contrast, the NSA engaged in bulk collection absent any reasonable suspicion that the individuals whose telephone information was being collected were engaged in any wrongdoing. Almost *all* of the information obtained bore *no* relationship whatsoever to criminal activity. The government nevertheless placed a pen register and trap-and-trace on all U.S. persons—essentially treating everyone in the United States as though they were Michael Lee Smith.

In *Smith*, moreover, the pen register captured only the phone numbers called by Smith. The bulk collection program, on the other hand, collected not just the telephone numbers dialed but also the numbers received and the trunk identifier information and session times. And it did this not just for a limited time but for months at a time. With this data, the government could build complex—and accurate—models of social interaction. The volume of information captured was not just more of the same. It represented a much greater intrusion into citizens' intimate relationships and private lives.

The dissent in *Smith* recognized that single numbers could reveal content. Justice Stewart explained that telephone calls "easily could reveal the identities of the persons and the places called, and thus reveal the most intimate details of a person's life."[9] The problem is magnified in the current context. It is not just one, or a handful of such facts that can be learned about individuals, but *all* such calls and facts.

Trunk identifier information reveals not just the target of a particular telephone call but where the callers and receivers are located. In 1976, the police were only able to tell when Smith was at home. The telephone did not follow him around. Mobile technologies now allow the police to ascertain where people are when they connect to mobile networks. And the bulk collection of records means that the government has the ability to do that for not just one person but for virtually the entire population.

Further characteristics distinguish the case. In *Smith*, the telephone company consented to placing a pen register on the line. There was no element of compulsion. This is an important step in the legal analysis. The Fourth Amendment only applies to government actors. To the extent that companies are acting in their private capacity, the Fourth Amendment is not relevant. But in 1989, the Supreme Court considered a case in which a railroad company conducted drug testing on employees at the behest of the government. In *Skinner v. Railway Labor Executives Association*, the Court held that when private entities are compelled to act, they must be viewed as a government agent.

In the case of the telephony metadata program, the government compelled the telephone companies to produce all telephony metadata, under court order and with the threat of sanction for failing to abide by the terms of the secondary order. The telecommunication service providers acted at the behest of the government and, as such, were within the reach of the Fourth Amendment.

Perhaps the most important difference between the two situations lies in the realms of technology and social construction. The extent to which we rely on electronic communications to conduct our daily lives is of a fundamentally different scale and complexity than in the 1970s. As a result, the type of information that can be learned about not just individuals, but neighborhoods, churches, school boards, political parties, Girl Scout troops—indeed, any social, political, or economic network—simply by the placement of a pen register or trap and trace, is far beyond what the *Smith* Court confronted.

JUDICIAL TENSION: TRESPASS AND *KATZ*'S REASONABLE EXPECTATION OF PRIVACY

In *Katz v. United States*, the 1967 case in which law enforcement placed an electronic bug on the outside of a phone booth, the Supreme Court replaced physical trespass doctrine with one based on a reasonable expectation of privacy. The fact that the device used to record the gambler's conversation "did not happen to penetrate the wall of the phone booth," the Court wrote, "can have no constitutional significance."[10] The Fourth Amendment protects against electronic violations, as much as physical intrusions, into protected spaces.

Katz was an effort by the Court to come to terms with new technologies. We again find ourselves at a *Katz*-type moment.

We are confronted by surveillance techniques that may not physically intrude on the home but which profoundly implicate what Brandeis referred to as "the privacies of life."[11] Not only does the government gain penetrating insight into our private affairs, but it does so to a degree that even those engaged in the activity do not realize. That it is an electronic trespass, and not a physical one, matters little. As Brandeis stated, "It is not the breaking of his doors, and the rummaging of his drawers, that constitutes the essence of the offense; but it is the invasion of his indefeasible right of personal security, personal liberty and private property. . . ."[12] The digital trespass in which the NSA has engaged is not supported by probable cause. It is not supported by reasonable suspicion. No suspicion of any wrongdoing is contemplated by the collection of records.

In recent Fourth Amendment cases considering new technologies, a schism has appeared in the Court between adopting an approach based on traditional concepts of trespass on property, and examining the facts from the vantage of the reasonable expectation of privacy—a higher bar adopted in 1967 as a way of augmenting the Court's previous reliance on physical space. Under either approach, the metadata program fails constitutional muster.

In *United States v. Jones*, the Court considered a case involving 28-day surveillance. The government obtained a search warrant permitting it to place a Global-Positioning System (GPS) tracking device on a car registered to the wife of a suspected drug dealer. The day after the warrant expired, agents installed the device and followed the car's movements for nearly a month. Information obtained allowed the government to indict Antoine Jones and others on drug trafficking conspiracy charges. The Court held that attaching the GPS device to the car and tracing its movements amounted to a search within the meaning of the Fourth Amendment.

In *Jones*, the Court recognized that *Katz*'s reasonable expectation of privacy test did not supplant the rights in existence at the time the Fourth Amendment was forged. Justice Scalia, writing for the Court, underscored that it was important to be clear about what happened in the case: "The government physically occupied private property for the purpose of obtaining information. We have no doubt that such a physical intrusion would have been considered a 'search' within the meaning of the Fourth Amendment when it was adopted."[13] Scalia cited *Entick v. Carrington*, noting that the Court had described it as a "'monument of English freedom' 'undoubtedly familiar' to 'every American statesman' at the time the constitution was adopted, and considered to be 'the true and ultimate expression of constitutional law' with regard to search and seizure."[14] He continued, "At bottom, we must 'assur[e] preservation of that degree of privacy against government that existed when the Fourth Amendment was adopted.'"[15]

The Court rejected a reading of *Katz* that would reduce the rights established at the Founding. "[A]t a minimum," Justice Scalia wrote, the "18th-century guarantee against unreasonable searches . . . must provide . . . the degree of protection it afforded when it was adopted."[16]

The Fourth Amendment was introduced to prevent general warrants. *Katz* does not change the minimum requirements to make similar government action constitutional.

In *Jones*, a shadow majority recognized the unique challenges of a digital age. In separate opinions, five justices indicated unease with the intrusiveness of modern technology, endorsing a mosaic theory of privacy. Justice Alito, joined by Justices Ginsburg, Breyer, and Kagan, suggested that in most criminal investigations, long-term monitoring impinges on expectations of privacy. The nature of new technologies matters: "Recent years have seen the emergence of many new devices that permit the monitoring of a person's movements. In some locales, closed-circuit television video monitoring is becoming ubiquitous." The Court continued, "On toll roads, automatic toll collection systems create a precise record of the movements of motorists who choose to make use of their convenience. Many motorists purchase cars that are equipped with devices that permit a central station to ascertain the car's location at any time so that roadside assistance may be provided if needed and the car may be found if it is stolen."[17]

The daily business of living one's life creates a digital record with privacy implications. "Perhaps most significant," Justice Alito added, "cell phones and other wireless devices now permit wireless carriers to track and record the location of users—and as of June 2011, it has been reported, there were more than 322 million wireless devices in use in the United States."[18] Before computers, practicality proved one of the greatest protectors of individual privacy. It was difficult and expensive to conduct long-term surveillance. But technology has changed the equation. The government is able to engage in long-term surveillance. While relatively short-term monitoring of movement in public space, such as a police officer physically following an individual, might be consistent with the Fourth Amendment, "the use of longer term GPS monitoring in investigations of most offenses impinges on expectations of privacy."[19]

Justice Sotomayor went further than Justice Alito, calling into question the entire basis for the third-party doctrine. In light of the level of intrusiveness represented by modern technology, "it may be necessary to reconsider the premise that an individual has no reasonable expectation of privacy in information voluntarily disclosed to third parties."[20] She pointed out that the third-party approach "is ill suited to the digital age, in which people reveal a great deal of information about themselves to third parties in the course of carrying out mundane tasks." Justice Sotomayor continued, "People disclose the phone numbers that they dial or text to the cellular providers; the URLs that they visit and the e-mail addresses with which they correspond to their Internet service providers; and the books, groceries, and medications they purchase to online retailers." She added, "I would not assume that all information voluntarily disclosed to some member of the public for a limited purpose is, for that reason alone, disentitled to Fourth Amendment protection."[21]

In another case, *Kyllo v. United States*, the Court considered whether thermal scanning—another novel technology—conducted outside of a target's home constituted a search within the meaning of the Fourth Amendment. Agents, having picked up a heat signature that suggested that grow lights were being used inside the target's garage, used the information to obtain a search warrant. Although the case turned on physical trespass, both the majority and the dissent emphasized the importance of taking account of the impact of new technologies on the privacy interests at stake.

Justice Scalia delivered the opinion of the Court: "It would be foolish to contend," he wrote, "that the degree of privacy secured to citizens by the Fourth Amendment has been entirely unaffected by the advance of technology." The question the Court confronted was "what limits there are upon this power of technology to shrink the realm of guaranteed privacy." Homeowners should not be left to "the mercy of advancing technology."[22]

For the dissent, homeowners lacked any reasonable expectation of privacy in heat emissions outside their domiciles. But even for the dissent, the sole issue was not the physical integrity of the home: "If such equipment did provide its user with *the functional equivalent of access to a private place*—such as, for example, the telephone booth involved in *Katz*, or an office building—then the rule should apply to such an area as well as a home."[23]

Electronic recordkeeping has become integral to the conduct of life in the 21st century. Digital communications are on a par with the role of the telephone that the Court considered in *Katz*. At that time, the Court explained, "One who occupies [a phone booth], shuts the door behind him, and pays the toll that permits him to place a call is surely entitled to assume that the words he utters into the mouthpiece will not be broadcast to the world. *To read the Constitution more narrowly is to ignore the vital role that the public telephone has come to play in private communication.*"[24]

Whatever role telephones played when *Katz* was decided in 1967, their integration into society has deepened in the intervening years. Digital communications are central to our lives. That we contract with companies to ensure careful treatment of our private information and that we use passwords to access our telephone, banking, and financial records online *is* the equivalent of shutting the door of the phone booth.

The courts are beginning to recognize privacy interests in this new, electronic sphere. In 2010, the Sixth Circuit held in

United States v. Warshak that the government had violated Steven Warshak's Fourth Amendment rights when it obtained e-mail from his Internet service provider absent a warrant based on probable cause. The court noted that Warshak had a reasonable expectation of privacy in his e-mail. *Warshak* dealt directly with content—the actual e-mails sent and received. At some point, metadata becomes content as well.

The government argues that even if one sets *Smith* aside and considers the collection of telephony metadata to be a search, it is nevertheless reasonable. As aforementioned, this claim understates the impact of new technologies, the potential insights yielded by novel forms of data analysis, and the intrusiveness of the Section 215 program. Even if citizens wanted to opt out of having metadata collected, it would be virtually impossible to do so. There have been advances in encryption, but for the most part, they revolve around content—not metadata. The only option would be not to use a telephone. Doing so, however, would mean divesting oneself of a role in the modern world—impacting one's social relationships, employment, and ability to conduct financial and personal affairs.

These considerations are narrowly focused on telephony metadata. The logic of the government's argument, however, has virtually no limit. Almost all forms of metadata could be at stake, ranging from education and financial records, to gun purchases and groceries. Americans have a contractual relationship with corporate entities, to whom they have entrusted parts of their lives, such as friendships, correspondence, and buying patterns. Creating a relationship with Safeway to obtain less expensive food is something different in kind than divulging to the government that you keep kosher, help to support your mother, or love chocolate.

A variant of the government's argument focuses on the distinction between the collection of information, on the one hand, and access to, or analysis of, the data, on the other. What makes the search reasonable in the first instance, it suggests, is that later access to the information must meet the standards of probable cause (or some variant thereof). In other words, the terms of subsequent use of the data alter the quality of the initial search. This argument is closely tied to the what can be termed the "haystack" argument.

THE PROVERBIAL NEEDLE IN THE HAYSTACK

Proponents of the metadata programs argue that to find threats, intelligence agencies must obtain, and then mine, all available data. The analogy that has been suggested is that the government must first build a haystack, in order to find the proverbial needle. Why? Some information can only be gleaned from, or understood in, a broader context. We may not know at the front end who is a member of a terrorist cell or who may be attempting to obtain weapons of mass destruction from traffickers, but once a graph of social networks has been constructed, clusters and connections can be identified that yield insight into these networks. Any person, moreover, could prove a threat to the United States—even where they may be only tangentially related to established networks. Therefore, everyone's data must be obtained.

For constitutional purposes, the argument continues, it is not a search within the meaning of the Fourth Amendment to use technology to construct the haystack. This occurs only when a person starts sifting through the hay to find the needle. Alternatively, even if it is a search at the moment of collection, ensuring that probable cause (or something approximating it) accompanies the subsequent query of the data renders the initial collection reasonable.

These arguments depend upon a distinction between collection of information and access to the data—as well as a relationship between the two. They do not withstand scrutiny.

First, the collection of information *is* a search. Consistent with *Katz*'s reasonable expectation of privacy test, it is access to the information that violates the private sphere. If the government were to mount a camera in your bedroom and to record everything that you do there—*promising* not to look at it unless it had a *really good reason* to do so—it would still be an invasion of your privacy. The violation is determined from the point of view of the individual subject to the incursion, not from the perspective of the entity doing the recording. It is at the moment that the information is obtained that the search occurs. When Lord Coke's trunks were brought to Charles I, and Entick, Leach, and Wilkes had their items seized and taken away for later inspection, the issue was not whether someone read the items at the moment they were seized. It was that the Crown gained access to them at all.

The privacy interests physically protected by sheet rock and stucco mirror the interests at stake in a digital realm. The only difference is that they now exist in a parallel universe in which we live our digital lives. The importance of solitude, the necessity of creating space for the evolution of ideas and self, the role of privacy in democratic deliberation and self-determination, the need to be able to create diversity in one's intimate relationships, and the impact of privacy incursions on other liberty rights, such as free association and free speech are all at stake at the moment the information is collected.

The reason why turns upon a simple truth: individuals change their behavior when what they do and say is monitored by the government. One is inherently *not* free when what one does, who one loves, with whom one shares one's passions, and what those passions are, are recorded by the government. What I disclose, on a limited basis, to Safeway, Amazon, or the local coffee house, for the provision of commercial services, is different from the government collecting this information, combining it with other data, and potentially using it to try to anticipate my behavior or to look for illegal activities. The same is true, for instance, of Google collecting data rather than the government. Google does not own guns. It cannot put me in prison. And it cannot impose the death penalty. The government can.

The overall level of coercion thus felt by the target of government surveillance, *even if the information is never read or analyzed*, is likely to be higher than that felt by a consumer contracting with a corporation for a limited purpose. Individuals, correspondingly, have a higher likelihood of altering their behavior when their private lives are exposed to government officials, thus impacting their rights. It is for this reason that the Fourth Amendment specifies that "The right of the people to be secure in their persons, houses, papers, and effects, against unreasonable search *and seizure,* shall not be violated."

In a *Huffington Post* article arguing against the constitutionality of the NSA bulk metadata collection program, Professor Geoffrey Stone, who served on the president's Review Board of the metadata collection program, added yet a further consideration. The costs associated with pen registers and trap-and-trace devices have, in the past, created a barrier to the government's use of the equipment. It has been time-consuming, fact specific, and costly, which has meant that, as a practical matter, the government could use this technique in only a handful of situations. The low risk of being targeted meant that individuals did not alter their expectation of privacy—or their behavior.

Technology has changed the calculation. Under the Section 215 interpretation, the government could collect metadata without the resource constraints that previously prevented it from placing all citizens under surveillance. Justice Alito brought out this point in *Jones* in relation to the use of GPS technologies. Technology should not continually erode our traditional expectations of privacy. As Stone observed, "Without that principle, the evolution of a 'Big Brother' government could do serious damage to the liberty, privacy and dignitary interests of the individual that are essential to a free society."[25]

A second problem with the haystack approach is that the Supreme Court has not recognized any "automation exception" to the Fourth Amendment. To the contrary, it is the moment at which the thermal device picks up the heat signature, when the GPS device is placed on the car, and when the dog sniffs the marijuana inside the home—not when the dog barks to alert his handler—that the search has occurred. In *United States v. Karo*, a case from the mid-1980s that turned on the use of a beeper to follow a suspected drug dealer's car, Justice Stevens explained: "The expectation of privacy should be measured from the standpoint of the citizen whose privacy is at stake, not of the government. It is compromised the moment the invasion occurs. A bathtub is a less private area when the plumber is present even if his back is turned."[26] The collection of the information *is* the intrusion into privacy.

This line of reasoning further ignores the intercession of human judgment throughout the process. It is a human being that decides to collect the information. Humans submit applications to FISC, grant applications, and issue primary and secondary orders to collect the data. Individuals program computers to collect and collate information. They write algorithms, replete with inbuilt assumptions and biases, and then decide where the information goes and in what form it will be available for others to see. People are involved throughout. To represent it otherwise is to ignore the extent to which technology is being used at the behest of government and not in its stead.

A third problem is that the collection-access divide assumes that the terms of the latter influence the former. That is, if the subsequent act is accompanied by probable cause (or something similar), then the collection itself is rendered reasonable. This argument, too, fails. For Fourth Amendment purposes, it is the collection itself that must meet the criteria. This does not mean that a similar analysis may not accompany access to, and analysis and use, of the data. A separate Fourth Amendment test must be applied. As is addressed in Chapter 7, a use restriction may thus accompany the way in which the government uses foreign intelligence—particularly with regard to criminal prosecution.

But wait, critics say. Imagine that the government has a time machine that enables it to go back in time to listen to past phone calls with probable cause and a warrant. What if, by doing so, *terrible* crimes could be prevented? Would that change the calculation? Under a balancing test, the interests at stake would be heightened. Would collection *then* be deemed reasonable?

There is little question that total information awareness could greatly reduce violence and threats to the government. Dictatorships and totalitarian regimes for centuries have operated on this premise. But if that is the kind of government we would like to have as a society, then that is a very different political order than the one envisioned by our Founders—and one directly at odds with the basic precepts and understandings of our Constitution. The question at that point is not whether it is a violation of the Fourth Amendment. It is whether we ought to have a Fourth Amendment at all.

Living constitutionalism requires the Court to adjust written principles to the times. In *McCulloch v. Maryland*, Chief Justice Marshall wrote, "We must never forget that it is a constitution we are expounding."[27] Just over a century later, Justice Brandeis recognized that in the intervening time, the Supreme Court had "repeatedly sustained the exercise of power by Congress, under various clauses of that instrument, over objects of which the Fathers could not have dreamed."[28] The Fourth Amendment was no exception. Its purpose was to protect the privacies of life. "But 'time works changes, brings into existence new conditions and purposes,'" Brandeis warned. "Subtler and more far-reaching means of invading privacy have become available to the government." He continued, "Discovery and invention have made it possible for the government, by means far more effective than stretching upon the rack, to obtain disclosure in court of what is whispered in the closet."[29]

Justice Brandeis's words have proved prescient. "The progress of science in furnishing the government with means of espionage is not likely to stop with wire-tapping," he wrote. "Ways may someday be developed by which the government, without removing papers from secret drawers, can reproduce them in court, and by which it will be enabled to expose to a jury the most intimate occurrences of the home." Brandeis noted, "Advances in the . . . sciences may bring means of exploring unexpressed beliefs, thoughts and emotions." He highlighted the importance of general warrants to the American Revolution and underscored the danger of allowing the government to use such technologies indiscriminately. "That it 'places the liberty of every man in the hands of every petty officer' was said by James Otis of much lesser intrusions than these. To Lord Camden, a far slighter intrusion seemed 'subversive of all the comforts of society.' Can it be that the Constitution affords no protection against such invasions of individual security?"[30]

The technologies at issue in the bulk collection programs invade citizens' privacy to an unprecedented degree. As Brandeis recognized, "As a means of espionage, writs of assistance and general warrants are but puny instruments of tyranny and oppression when compared with wire-tapping."[31] The wiretapping of a single individual, in turn, is but an equally puny instrument when compared with the collection and analysis of citizens' metadata, year in and year out, 24 hours a day, 7 days a week.

CHAPTER SEVEN

...

Reform

ONE OF THE best titles ever selected for an academic paper (admittedly, a low bar), was given by Stanford University Professor Scott Sagan to his 2004 examination of nuclear security. He studied the near meltdown at the Fermi reactor in Michigan in 1966, the 1986 space shuttle Challenger explosion, and the 1994 accidental targeting of two U.S. Army Black Hawk helicopters by Air Force pilots in Iraq, in the process observing that safety outlets built into organizational structures to increase reliability ended up backfiring. The conclusion that Professor Sagan reached is that the *more* protection one builds into a system, somewhat counterintuitively, the *less* secure it may become. A form of social shirking occurs: if enough other people or entities have their eye on the situation, individuals and groups may be less prone to take responsibility. Sagan entitled the piece, "The Problem of Redundancy Problem."[1]

Sagan's insight translates to foreign intelligence. Following the Snowden releases, the first response of many commentators was that the intelligence community needed *more* oversight. There were not enough people aware of what was going on, the argument ran. More eyes would solve the issue. While such an initial response is understandable, creating yet more oversight would not solve the underlying issues. If anything, there has been too much reliance on redundancy.

The 2008 FISA Amendments Act created myriad reporting requirements. At least twice a year, the attorney general and the Director of National Intelligence must assess compliance with Section 702 targeting and minimization procedures and submit the evaluation to the FISC, the House Permanent Select Committee on Intelligence and the Senate Select Committee on Intelligence, and the House and Senate Committees on the Judiciary. The inspectors general of both the Department of Justice and the agency using the authorities are authorized to review compliance with the targeting and minimization procedures. They are required to review the number of intelligence reports containing citizens' identities disseminated to other agencies and the number of targets later determined to be in the United States. They provide their reports to the attorney general, the Director of National Intelligence (DNI), and the same four congressional committees (intelligence and judiciary in both houses).

The head of each agency obtaining information, in addition, must annually review the programs to ascertain whether foreign information has been, or will be, obtained. The review must consider the number of disseminated reports containing citizens' information, the number of targets later found to be within domestic bounds, and the acquisition and minimization procedures approved by the DNI. The document is provided to the Foreign Intelligence Surveillance Court, the attorney general, the DNI, and the congressional committees.

Finally, every six months, the attorney general must inform the intelligence and judiciary committees of certifications submitted consistent with Section 702 (indicating the information sought was related to foreign intelligence), the reasons for exercising the authority, directives issued in conjunction with the acquisition, a description of judicial review (including copies of orders or pleadings submitted in connection with such reviews that contain a significant legal interpretation of the law), actions taken to challenge or enforce directives, compliance reviews, and a description of incidents of noncompliance.

Adding yet more oversight to this process would not resolve the underlying constitutional concerns. What would prove more effective? More *robust* oversight, a stronger distinction between criminal law and national security, and a fundamental rethinking of our nation's approach to foreign intelligence that takes account of the digital world in which we now live.

MORE ROBUST OVERSIGHT

The current oversight mechanisms are failing in important ways to limit the expansion of executive power. Some of the problems are relatively simple to address.

The Senate Select Committee on Intelligence (SSCI), for instance, as originally conceived, restricted the amount of time legislators could sit on the committee. The purpose was to avoid agency capture, a form of corruption where agencies entrusted with acting in the public interest end up advancing the interests of the entity they are supposed to be monitoring. In 2004, SSCI eliminated term limits, with the result that some members have been embedded in the intelligence infrastructure for 15 years or more. When the Snowden releases first occurred, some senators went on the road, defending the executive branch's actions. It was hardly an appropriate role for an oversight body charged with a watchdog function. Restoring term limits could help to ensure that Congress casts a more critical eye on executive branch activities—and that more members of Congress participate, making oversight more representative.

Other problems, such as those stemming from the design and evolution of the FISC, may be more difficult to fix. But they would be important steps forward. In particular, the court's deference to the executive and the absence of either technology experts or adversarial counsel have weakened the rigor of the court's review.

Scholars have noted that the success rate for applications under traditional FISA is "unparalleled in any other American court." Over the first two and a half decades, FISC approved nearly every application without any modification. Between 1979 and 2003, FISC denied only 3 out of 16,450 applications. In the last decade, FISC has ruled on 18,473 applications for electronic surveillance and physical search (2003–2008), and electronic surveillance (2009–2012). Although some were withdrawn prior to the court's ruling, FISC only denied 8 in whole and 3 in part. FISC has *never* denied an application for an order under Section 215.[2]

The impact of the court's deference is concerning. In the aftermath of 9/11, FISC secretly began approving bulk collection, with the result that even one of the orders could collect billions of telephone records. Congress, not anticipating the expansion of targeting to allow for bulk collection, included language in the original statute *requiring* FISC to grant applications once the statutory conditions are met. The combination—FISC's deference, the secret redefinition of "relevant" to mean "anything that might possibly be helpful," and the statutory language *requiring* the order to be granted—acted together to undermine citizens' constitutional protections.

As a structural matter, Congress tried to create an even-handed, neutral arbiter by requiring that FISC judges be selected by the chief justice of the Supreme Court from at least seven different federal districts. The judges serve staggered terms of up to seven years, and, having once served, become ineligible for further service. To ensure diversity, any federal district court judge may be selected. The chief justice selects all of the judges on the Foreign Intelligence Surveillance Court of Review (FISCR).

Despite efforts to ensure diversity, appointments have not reflected the breadth of the political spectrum. To the extent that ideology is reflected in the appointments process, the court has been heavily weighted toward one side. The past two chief justices were appointed by Republican presidents, and they tended to select judges nominated by Republican administrations. When the Snowden documents were released, only 1 of the 11 judges serving on FISC had been a Democratic nominee to the bench. Over the previous decade, of the 20 judges appointed to FISC and FISCR, only 3 had been Democratic nominees.

According to the public record, FISCR has only met twice: once in 2002 and once in 2008. On both occasions, the panels consisted entirely of Republican appointees, some of whom had publicly argued that FISA was an unconstitutional usurpation of executive power. Judge Laurence Silberman of the DC Circuit testified to Congress in 1978 that the legislation violated the Constitution. Silberman, who had previously served as deputy attorney general, was "absolutely convinced that the administration bill, if passed, would be an enormous and fundamental mistake which the Congress and the American people would have reason to regret."[3] For Silberman, the judiciary's role in national security surveillance should be circumscribed. His chief concern was not an "imperial presidency," but the advent of an "imperial judiciary." He considered the authorities ascribed to FISC to be an unconstitutional erosion of executive power. Another FISCR judge, Ralph Guy, similarly argued as a U.S. attorney for the government in *U.S. v. U.S. District Court* that the president did not need a warrant for national security surveillance.

Along with Judge Leavy, a Reagan appointee, Judges Silberman and Guy heard the first appeal in the history of FISA—issuing the decision that brought down the wall between national security and law enforcement. The FISCR panel that created a foreign intelligence exception to the Fourth Amendment warrant requirement similarly lacked a diverse political base. It included Chief Judge Bruce Selya and Senior Circuit Judges Ralph Winter and Morris Arnold—appointees of Presidents Ronald Reagan and George H. W. Bush.

To the extent that appointments stand in as a proxy for ideologies, such as greater deference to the executive, the lack of diversity in the appointments process—especially in light of the far-reaching, secret decisions issued by the court—raises serious questions about the extent to which FISC is serving as neutral arbiter, much less a check on executive power.

The deference exhibited by FISC with regard to traditional FISA has, if anything, become more pronounced in regard to new technologies. Over the past decade, the court has abdicated some of its responsibilities by giving the NSA the power to decide whom to target and what to do with the information. When judges discovered that the agency had lied, or misled it, FISC admonished the NSA, but, for the most part, allowed it to keep the information and to continue collection.

Recall that in 1998 Congress introduced the business records provision, requiring that the government submit a statement of "specific and articulable facts" in support of its application. Although the showing was eliminated in 2001, four years later Congress reintroduced a requirement that the government submit a statement of facts establishing "reasonable grounds to believe that the tangible things" to be obtained are "relevant to an authorized investigation." This language put FISC in the position of verifying whether the government has met its burden of proof prior to obtaining intelligence.

The court, however, stopped serving in this function. Its primary order authorizing the collection of telephony metadata required that designated *NSA officials* make a finding that there is "reasonable, articulable suspicion" (RAS) that a seed identifier proposed for query is associated with a particular foreign terrorist organization prior to its use. It was left to the executive to determine whether it had sufficient evidence to conduct surveillance.

The dangers associated with FISC removing itself from the process are clear. For nearly three years, the NSA did not follow these procedures, even though officials were aware of the violation. It was not until early 2009 that the illegal behavior was brought to the court's attention. The DOJ informed FISC that the government had been querying the business records in a manner that contravened the original order and sworn statements of several executive branch officials.

FISC was not amused. Judge Reggie Walton expressed concern "about what appears to be a flagrant violation of its Order in this matter."[4] The NSA had repeatedly misled FISC in its handling of the database. FISC issued an order directing a comprehensive review of the telephony metadata program. It gave the government until February 17, 2009, to file a brief to defend its actions and to help FISC to determine whether further action should be taken against the government.

The NSA initially admitted only "that NSA's descriptions to [FISC] of the alert list process ... were inaccurate and that the Business Records Order did not provide the Government with authority to employ the alert list in the manner in which it did." The agency acknowledged that the majority of the identifiers associated with the alert list were not supported by reasonable, articulable suspicion, as the court had required. The actual numbers, reported to FISC in February 2009, were staggering: as of January 15, 2009, only 1,935 of the 17,835 identifiers on the alert list were RAS approved.[5]

It was not that the NSA was unaware of the requirements established by the statute and by FISC. The attorney general had, consistent with the primary order, established minimization procedures that laid out the process that the NSA was required to follow. Nevertheless, apparently, neither the Signals Intelligence Directorate nor the Office of General Counsel had caught the fact that nearly 90 percent of the queries to the bulk dataset had been illegal. Nor had they realized that their reports to FISC claiming that only RAS-approved numbers were being run against the bulk metadata were false. Meanwhile, the NSA had disseminated 275 reports to the FBI resulting from contact chaining and queries of the telephony metadata.

Despite these violations, the government argued that FISC should neither rescind nor modify its order. The court allowed the program to continue.

The January 2009 incident is far from the first—or only—time that the NSA acted outside the scope of its authority. In September 2006, the NSA's inspector general expressed concern that the agency was collecting more data under Section 215 than FISC had authorized. The agency had been obtaining 16-digit credit card numbers as well as names contained in the records of operator-assisted calls. In October 2008, the government reported to the court that, after FISC authorized the NSA to increase the number of analysts working with the business records metadata and had directed that the NSA train the newly authorized analysts, 31 (out of 85) analysts queried the business records metadata *without even being aware that they were doing so*. Despite taking corrective steps, two months later the government notified FISC that an analyst had not installed a modified access tool and, as a result, had again queried the data using identifiers for which no RAS standard had been satisfied. Just over a month later, the government informed FISC that between December 10, 2008, and January 23, 2009, two analysts had used 280 foreign telephone identifiers to query the business records metadata without first establishing RAS.

Numerous further misstatements and incidents of noncompliance occurred. But instead of rescinding the NSA's authority, FISC allowed the agency to continue collection *and* to keep the data illegally obtained. It is not that the court was not upset by the NSA's bad behavior. But it did not penalize the NSA for breaking the law. The court failed to provide a remedy for the violation of citizens' rights.

Part of the problem stems from a lack of understanding of technology. The issue here is one of design. Although FISC has legal advisors, it lacks independent experts who can advise the judges with regard to the technologies in question. Throughout the noncompliance incidents, the FISC judges do not appear to have understood how the NSA's procedures and algorithms worked. Nor did the court seem to grasp what information had been incorporated into different databases, or whether they had been subjected to the appropriate analysis before data mining. Adding a pool of experts would decrease the court's reliance on the intelligence agencies, who are hardly disinterested observers where their own interests are involved. It would help FISC to get up to speed on rapidly evolving technologies. It would perform a translation function for the information provided by the agencies. And it would assist the court in crafting the right questions to ensure that the orders are being followed.

Paired with the lack of independent technological expertise has been the absence of adversarial counsel, who could argue before the court and against the executive branch on behalf of citizens' rights. This function is especially important since FISC, operating in secret, has begun to engage in statutory and constitutional interpretation.

In 2002, for instance, FISCR suggested in *In Re Directives* that the case raised "important questions of statutory interpretation, and constitutionality" and concluded "that FISA, as amended by the Patriot Act, supports the government's position, and that the restrictions imposed by the FISA court are not required by FISA or the Constitution."[6] Similarly, in August 2013, FISC issued a 29-page Amended Memorandum Opinion on the FBI's application for the telephony metadata program. Appending the 17-page order to the opinion, Judge Eagan considered Fourth Amendment jurisprudence, the statutory language of Section 215, and the canons of statutory construction to justify granting the order.

Not only is FISC ruling on complex statutory and constitutional questions, but the court is drawing from its past decisions as precedent, in the process developing a jurisprudence that appears to be binding on future courts. The government, moreover, has begun to cite to previous FISC decisions as persuasive legal authority. This is not at all what Congress envisioned when it made provision for a new court to determine whether the government had met the requirements of probable cause, and to verify that the appropriate certifications had been made.

That the court is creating a new body of jurisprudence *absent any adversarial counsel* is of even greater concern. It affects the quality of the argument. It also means that there is no one who can appeal the secret findings of the court when the opinion favors the government position. This is a particularly pressing concern, because at times FISC's interpretations have gone beyond Supreme Court doctrine, laying out new exceptions to the Fourth Amendment.

In 2008, for example, FISC broadened the "special needs" exception to the warrant requirement to apply to foreign intelligence data collection. The U.S. Supreme Court has *never* recognized such an exception. Nevertheless, the decision became established precedent. In *In re Directives*, FISCR looked back at its 2002 decision in *In re Sealed Case* to confirm "the existence of a foreign intelligence exception to the warrant requirement." It acknowledged that FISCR had "avoided an express holding that a foreign intelligence exception exists by assuming arguendo [for the sake of argument] that whether or not the warrant requirements were met, the statute could survive on reasonableness grounds." FISCR went on to determine that, as an appellate court, it would "review findings of fact for clear error and legal conclusions (including determinations about the ultimate constitutionality of government searches or seizures) de novo."[7] It then asserted, *for the first time*, a foreign intelligence surveillance exception to the Fourth Amendment. The court analogized the exception to the 1989 Supreme Court consideration of the warrantless drug testing of railway workers (*Skinner v. Railway Labor Executives' Association*). The government's need to respond to an overriding public danger could justify a minimal intrusion on privacy. The government later cited *In re Directives* in its August 9, 2013, white paper, defending the telephony metadata program, in support of an exception to the Fourth Amendment warrant requirement.

In sum, a separate body of secret law has evolved in ways not anticipated by Congress in 1978. It has been developed in in camera, ex parte proceedings, and serves as precedent for future judicial rulings. There is no right of appeal for individuals impacted by the court's rulings. Indeed, the decisions are not challengeable in open court, despite their direct impact on citizens' constitutional rights.

The solution does not appear to be to deny FISC the ability to engage in statutory or constitutional interpretation. It would be difficult to conceive of the court as addressing statutory questions *without* interpreting both the language and looking to the deeper constitutional questions. Moreover, as technology daily evolves, it is all but inevitable that many of the questions presented will raise important statutory and constitutional issues.

Constitutional advocates are needed, to give free rein to the important questions that accompany foreign intelligence authorities. The government's position should be challengeable, and appeal possible, with the Supreme Court acting as the final court.

The USA Freedom Act, which entered into law in June 2015, went some way toward addressing the problem. It required the Court to appoint at least five people within 180 days, to serve as amici curiae to FISC. Their function, as "friends of the court," will be to consider difficult questions that arise, particularly when new or emerging forms of surveillance present themselves. But many details still need to be addressed to ensure the independence and effectiveness of those selected for the panel.

It has yet to be determined, for example, how frequently amici will participate in questions before the court. In light of the absence of counsel for the past decade, in the course of which sensitive constitutional questions have presented themselves, one of the first responsibilities of counsel would be to review the current state of affairs and to submit arguments to the court, as appropriate, focused on past interpretations. Where programs are continued at three-month to yearly intervals, there are opportunities for rehearing.

As new technologies or novel questions present themselves, participation by amici will be essential. Determining when this is the case, however, is a difficult question. In 2010 Presiding Judge John D. Bates issued revised Rules of Procedure for FISC, requiring the government to inform the court, in writing, of the nature and significance of any new issues, including (but not limited to), novel questions of technology or law. Bates stipulated that the memorandum—submitted *prior* to seeking authorization for surveillance—explain the technique to be used, the circumstances for likely implementation of the technique, any legal issues raised, and the proposed minimization procedures to be applied.[8]

Bates's rule was an important step forward. In light of the incremental evolution of technology, however, it may be difficult for the NSA to identify precisely when such a threshold has been crossed. A lesson on point can be drawn from the example of the FBI's Next

Generation Identification (NGI) system. NGI allows for the collection of citizens' biometric data including millions of photos from the Interstate Photo System (IPS). The FBI considered the insertion of video surveillance feeds into IPS to have the same privacy implications as still pictures—despite the expansion of the database to incorporate new sources, audio recording, and continuous monitoring.[9]

One potential way to address this problem from within the NSA might be to use budget meetings as trigger points, incorporating a legal analysis into consideration of any new projects. That is, at the inception of any new project, the agency could be required to address the related legal questions. This analysis could then become linked to the technologies when they become operational and forwarded to FISC along with any applications. Another approach might be to insert a similar process into the technology certification regime, when information is transferred to new systems. Alternatively, internal procedures could trigger a report when new interpretations of statutory language arise within the Office of General Counsel. As a general rule, anything impacting the scope of collection or resulting in the generation of new knowledge should be considered as potentially within the reach of Rule 11, as modified by Judge Bates.

Notably, these alterations rely on the intelligence agencies to police themselves—a problematic proposition, as demonstrated by the NSA's repeated failure to ensure even that reasonable, articulable suspicion accompany database queries. Therefore, a secondary review of government applications, by the court's legal advisors, amici and technologists, could help to ensure that any issues that the government fails to brief are brought to the court's attention.

With Sagan's admonition about redundancy in mind, if adopted, the system would have to be constructed in such a way as to prevent any up-front social shirking by the government—perhaps by imposing a back-end cost should the judges, their legal advisors, or the amici, in conjunction with the technologists, find unreported issues.

The degree of transparency that will accompany any new processes is also less than clear. Certainly, there are programs that the government ought not to make public—this is the nature of foreign intelligence collection. As was recognized at the start of this book, from the earliest days of the Republic, U.S. national security has depended upon obtaining information and doing so in a way that does not unduly alert adversaries to our knowledge or sources.

But transparency also serves a vital function in a democratic state. Setting sources and methods to one side, at a minimum, legal analyses of statutory provisions and constitutional law should be made public. The court, government, and amici should be given the opportunity to consider this question and to recommend declassification of the legal questions and public discourse on legal issues. For the executive branch, on matters involving the interpretation of the law, the presumption should be in favor of disclosure. Along these lines, in 2014 President Obama announced that he was directing the Director of National Intelligence, in consultation with the attorney general, annually to review future FISC opinions with broad privacy implications, with an eye toward declassifying them. This is a welcome step in the right direction, although not, by itself, sufficient. What needs to be worked out is a dialogue between the Court, the intelligence agencies, and amici, to act in the best interests of the nation as a whole. Congressional committees similarly have a vital role to play.

It is hard to see how the debate that we have been having as a country since the Snowden releases could not have been held before—or that we would have been better served not having it. These are critical decisions being made in secret, with sobering implications for citizens' rights. They deserve to be adequately aired, debated, and discussed. There is still a significant way to go. It matters, for instance, what "derived from" Section 702 collection means. Ordinary citizens could be imprisoned or executed based on information obtained from foreign intelligence. They have the right to be able to challenge evidence obtained against them in a meaningful way. DOJ, however, has continued to classify its legal understanding of the term, in the process subverting the rule of law.

Numerous other details, such as what appellate mechanisms will be put into place, what resources will be available to the court, and how the amici panel operates, similarly have to be worked out. It is critical that the new institution be incorporated directly into the heart of the foreign intelligence procedure so that the court, and the country, will benefit.

PROTECTING RIGHTS: CRIMINAL LAW VERSUS NATIONAL SECURITY

One of the most important steps that could be taken to address the constitutional issues is to restore the distinction between criminal law and national security. It is essential for the future of individual rights—including not just the Fourth Amendment right to privacy, but also the First Amendment rights to association, religion, and free speech; the Second Amendment right to bear arms; and the Fifth Amendment right to due process—that we provide clear lines between law enforcement and foreign intelligence collection. Where overlap is inevitable, it should be cabined to prevent national security creep into ordinary criminal law.

The first step along this road would be to re-erect the FISA wall. The point of cementing the DOJ's Office of Intelligence Policy and Review into the process was, in part, to create a bottleneck that would prevent prosecutors from using the looser standards of foreign intelligence gathering to get around criminal law. The idea was to create an opportunity for prosecution where necessary, while not opening the floodgates to using foreign intelligence tools in lieu of law enforcement authorities.

Along these lines, the 2002 FISCR ruling in *In re Sealed Case* is deeply problematic. The *Truong* test that previously marked this realm—that the primary ends of intelligence gathering must be for foreign intelligence—should remain the standard (see Chapter 1). There is a basic logic at work here: if foreign intelligence gathering allows for weaker Fourth Amendment standards to be applied, then the information obtained should be primarily for foreign intelligence purposes, not for criminal law. This argument does not assume that the information should not be collected in the first place. It underscores that the purpose for which it is collected should be the purpose for which it is used.

Currently, the FBI is querying foreign intelligence databases for unrelated purposes. There are no limits on the types of criminal charges they can bring, based on information gathered under FISA. This practice should be ended. Any query of foreign intelligence databases should be accompanied by a warrant where citizens' information is involved. The reasons for not returning to FISC to obtain an order to query Section 702 data are far from clear, while the government's failure to do so is deeply problematic from a constitutional perspective.

In accordance with the Supreme Court's holding in *United States v. Verdugo-Urquidez*, non-U.S. citizens located abroad, who do not have a substantial relationship with the country, fall outside the contours of the Fourth Amendment. To the extent, then, that Section 702 targets non-U.S. citizens overseas *who lack a substantial connection*, there are minimal constitutional questions with the provision.

The problem is that it is not just noncitizen information being collected. To the contrary, the amount of U.S. persons' data swept up in the collection is so massive that the government cannot even estimate the numbers involved. Two important observations follow: first, *data is not tied to geography*; and second, communications entering and leaving the country *are* likely to involve citizens.

Because of the former, domestic communications may become swept up in collection, even as citizens' private documents, held on servers or routed overseas, may become subject to government surveillance. So even if citizens are not being targeted, their information may become subject to inspection. Eliminating "about" communications from upstream collection would get at part of the problem. But it would not address the mass monitoring of citizens' international communications and inadvertent storage of documents overseas.

As for the latter, until the 2008 FISA Amendments Act, the government did not have to approach a court to place U.S. citizens abroad under surveillance. This was one of the most important changes that Congress put into place with the addition of Sections 703 and 704. The way in which Section 702 is being used, though, allows the government to bypass some of these requirements, with the result that it cannot even provide a total of the number of Americans subject to surveillance. In light of modern technology, there may be no good way around this. But that makes it all the more important to draw a line between the foreign intelligence and criminal prosecution.

One way to distinguish the two realms would be by requiring the government to approach a court for a warrant before querying the data for criminal investigations. Here it is worth noting that none of the reasons presented by the government for bypassing the warrant requirement for foreign intelligence purposes are present when information is already held by U.S. officials.

In 2002, for instance, FISCR carved out a foreign intelligence exception to the warrant clause where (a) the purpose of surveillance went beyond "garden-variety" law enforcement; (b) the government's interest was "particularly intense"; and (c) there was a "high degree of probability that requiring a warrant would hinder the government's ability to collect time-sensitive information and, thus, would impede the vital national security interests that are at stake."[10] In 2000, the Southern District of New York similarly highlighted practical challenges as a reason for such exception. In *United States v. Bin Laden*, the court looked to the intricacies of foreign intelligence acquisition, the difficulty of predicting the international impact of seeking a warrant, the problem of foreign intelligence officials being seen as complicit, and the danger of notifying enemies by alerting foreign officials to U.S. actions.

These objections do not stand up to scrutiny when information is held by the United States. FISC is set up to allow for the swift granting of orders when the need arises. There are emergency exceptions, which require the government to go to the court within 48 hours. There is little reason why it should not be required to do so when citizens' information is involved. The intricacy of obtaining the information is no longer of issue, and there is no international impact. Nor are foreign officials involved, which means that prosecutors seeking a warrant do not alert other countries or our enemies to U.S. actions.

As a constitutional matter, moreover, it does not follow that simply because the information has been lawfully obtained, the government has the authority to search the data. Nearly 20 years ago, Professor Harold Krent proposed a use restriction for Fourth Amendment doctrine. His thesis was that the reasonableness of the seizure extends beyond the immediate acquisition of the information to the use subsequently made of the data so obtained. He argued that control over private information does not cease upon others' access. Reasonableness is not to be determined at one point in time, but at any time law enforcement authorities seek to make use of the property and information thus obtained. Use restrictions naturally follow.

The Fourth Amendment allows for line drawing between obtaining, searching, and further query of information. One case illustrating this point is *United States v. Ganias*, a Second Circuit case involving search of information copied from a hard drive, two years after it was obtained, for purposes other than that for which it was initially seized. The court held unconstitutional the retention and further examination of the data, despite the fact that law enforcement had returned to a judge to obtain a warrant. In *Riley v. California*, the Supreme Court addressed a similar situation in the context of a search incident to arrest, finding in 2014 that even where a cell phone has been legally seized, subsequent query of the device requires judicial intervention in the form of a warrant.

One counterargument that could be offered is that foreign intelligence often bleeds over into criminal law. That is, when we look for threats to the United States, the actions in question are already illegal. Espionage, bombing, shooting, and acts of terrorism are all crimes. It would be shortsighted for us to not allow ourselves to respond through the ordinary judicial process. A way to address this concern might be to limit the purpose for which the data could be accessed and used to a series of enumerated offenses, closely linked to foreign intelligence concerns.

In addition to policing the line between criminal law and national security, and inserting judicial review into the process, further thought needs to be given to how information derived from Section 702 is used in criminal prosecution. In February 2013 the Supreme Court accepted the government's argument in *Clapper v. Amnesty International* that the proper time for constitutional challenge to the statute is when DOJ informs criminal defendants that it plans to use information derived from Section 702 during trial.[11] Exactly when information counts as being "derived from" Section 702 is thus of great importance. But DOJ refuses to release the information. The definition must be made public and open to challenge. Documents leaked by Edward Snowden, which indicate that the government engages in parallel construction (directing law enforcement agencies to re-create an evidentiary trail so as to masque the fact that Section 702 was the original source of the information that led to prosecution), raise further concerns about how data is being handled. Greater transparency and more robust checks on how foreign intelligence information is used in criminal law are required.

LIVING IN A DIGITAL WORLD

The evolution of technology has had a profound impact on how information is generated, transferred, and stored. New types of data are available. Novel analytical tools allow for deeper insight into traditional and emerging forms of information. And resource limitations are falling away. It is becoming cheaper and less resource intensive to collect and analyze information about people. The 1979 decision in *Smith v. Maryland* concerning pen registers fails to acknowledge the world in which we now live. What is needed is a new constitutional rule of construction that acknowledges the deeper privacy interests involved.

Over the past four decades, the law has recognized three primary forms of information: content, personally identifiable information (PII), and business records. Each category enjoys a different level of protection. The Supreme Court applies a higher level to content and, in the context of third-party doctrine, a lower level to records held by companies. Accordingly, traditional FISA incorporates a more stringent regime for electronic surveillance and physical search, and less austere demands for pen registers and trap-and-trace devices. As new technologies have emerged in the post-9/11 environment, there have been efforts to apply the rules accompanying these categories to new areas. They are ill suited to the task. The privacy interests within each area and the new types of information that now exist have fundamentally transformed the world.

Continued reliance on outmoded approaches risks the privacy interests at stake. Personal information, for instance, is understood to relate to a single individual. This category includes information correlated with one person, such as a social security number, a home address, a credit card number, medical records, insurance information, or educational records. But new technologies have extended the category to include areas such as biometric markers, habit identification, and pattern matching—all of which are more intrusive than, for instance, one's home address.

In the past, the law has relied on stripping PII from records as a way to protect privacy. Yet in light of advances in computer science, research has shown the ease with which records can be reidentified with particular people. A 2015 study conducted at the Massachusetts Institute of Technology, for instance, examined three months of credit card records for 1.1 million people. Researchers found that only four publicly available spatiotemporal points were sufficient to reidentify 90 percent of the people.[12]

Business records relate to information generated in the process of buying or selling goods or services. They have traditionally been seen as less invasive than PII. But a tremendous amount of insight about individuals' private lives can be gleaned from third-party information. Indeed, entirely new categories of information have emerged.

Relational data, for instance, is a function of digitized social networks. Using visual and mathematical tools, technologists can map and analyze flows between people, groups, organizations, and geographic regions. Social network analytics provide insight into connections between individuals and their roles within and between groups: who are the key connectors, leaders, bridges, and isolates; where the key clusters are and who comprises them; who is in the core of the network; and who is on the periphery.

In an age of mobile and tracking technologies, another type of information has emerged: locational data. In some sense, it always existed. Police could always place a tail on a suspect. But the resource constraints that previously attended have all but fallen away. Locational data is now almost continuously generated by individuals as they go about their daily lives. This information is recorded and can be accessed relatively easily and without the expense traditionally involved.

At some point, these types of information morph into content—an area the Supreme Court has traditionally given the highest level of protection. Simultaneously, technology has expanded the amount of content available. More of our ideas, beliefs, and thoughts are digitized and made available through data analytics than ever before.

In short, we are at a *Katz*-type moment. Modern technologies are radically changing the world around us and creating digital doppelgangers who look and act exactly like us. Access to these other selves carries deep privacy implications, regardless of who holds the data. A new judicial test is needed to protect the values of the Fourth Amendment.

A rule of construction that interprets text to mean the *opposite* of what it meant when it was adopted does not pass constitutional muster. At a minimum, then, a new Fourth Amendment test must recognize the rejection of general warrants that marked the Founding. So, too, must the privacy interests originally at stake be protected.

In addition, a new judicial test will need to take account of the intrusiveness of the surveillance—not merely in physical terms, or as defined by who holds the data, but as an aspect of the privacy interests implicated. Data—including metadata—appertains to the individual about whom the information relates. Locational information, insight into relationships, and the content of individuals' communications all shed light on the private sphere. Traditional reliance on physical markers, such as the curtilage of the home, is not sufficient. Where intrusions are significant, a warrant must be required prior to collection.

Central to the calculation is the length of the surveillance and whether it is for past records or for ongoing monitoring. Whether the information is recorded, how long the information is kept, with whom it is shared, and how it is used—including whether it is being combined with other data to generate deeper insight into individuals' lives—matters. Finally, individuals whose information is collected, and who are subjected to criminal prosecution, should have an appropriate opportunity to challenge the authorities under which the government operates.

CONCLUDING REMARKS

In the late 1970s, the three branches of government renegotiated the boundaries of foreign intelligence collection to ensure that the government could obtain information about threats to U.S. national security. FISA was to be the sole means via which electronic surveillance could be conducted on domestic soil. But with the exogenous shock to the system in 2001, the framing suddenly altered. The executive branch went outside the agreement reached by the three branches. Then it renegotiated the boundaries and reinterpreted the statutory language to give itself greater leeway.

The problem is that the system is now radically out of balance. Restrictions have been rolled back. The amount and type of information available has expanded. Geographic borders no longer provide the same level of protection, and institutional boundaries no longer hold. The CIA, which was previously restricted from collecting intelligence within the United States, now sits on Joint Terrorism Task Forces and has access to entirely domestic conversations. The FBI, in turn, can use foreign intelligence authorities to collect information even when investigations are primarily criminal in nature. And law enforcement may query foreign intelligence databases that contain citizens' e-mails, telephone conversations, texts, and documents stored on the cloud, to find evidence of ordinary, domestic criminal activity, without any prior suspicion of wrongdoing.

As the division between criminal law and national security has collapsed, citizens' rights have been deeply impacted. It is more than just the right to privacy. Freedom of association, speech, and religion, and due process are also affected by the shifts in national security law, even as the accumulation of information in the executive branch threatens the separation of powers.

Foreign intelligence collection must continue. National security depends upon it.

But traditional models for collection based on geography (whether the object, device, or target is located within domestic bounds or outside the country), or whether information is being held by a third party, rather miss the point of what it is we are trying to protect.

What is needed is more *robust* oversight, a stronger distinction between criminal law and national security, and a thoughtful reframing of Fourth Amendment doctrine. There are strong reasons that the Founders rejected general warrants—reasons as powerful today as they were at the inception of the country. It is time to jettison a third-party doctrine that undergirds the ubiquitous collection of private information. A more effective approach, to guard the rights articulated in the Fourth Amendment, turns on use restrictions for information obtained for foreign intelligence purposes. At risk are the future of individual rights in the United States, the distribution of power across the federal government, and the relationship between federal entities and state and local government. The stakes could not be higher as we enter the digital age.

Notes

. . .

INTRODUCTION

1. 8 The Writings of George Washington From The Original Manuscript Sources, 1745–1799 479 (John C. Fitzpatrick ed., 1931).

2. Michael Isikoff, *NBC Reporter Recalls Exposing FBI Spying*, NBC News, Jan. 8, 2014, NBC News, *available at* http://www.nbcnews.com/news/investigations/nbc-reporter-recalls-exposing-fbi-spying-n5901.

3. Seymour M. Hersh, *Huge C.I.A. Operation Reported in U.S. Against Antiwar Forces, Other Dissidents in Nixon Years*, N.Y. Times, Dec. 22, 1974, at 1.

4. *Intelligence Activities: Hearing on the National Security Agency and Fourth Amendment Rights, U.S. Senate Select Committee to Study Governmental Operations with Respect to Intelligence Activities*, 94th Cong. at 1 (1975) (Statement of Sen. Frank Church, Chairman), *available at* http://www.aarclibrary.org/publib/church/reports/vol5/html/ChurchV5_0003a.htm.

5. *Intelligence Activities: Hearing on S. Res. 21 Before the Select Comm. to Study Governmental Operations with Respect to Intelligence Activities of the United States*, 94th Cong. ii (1975), at 36.

6. *Id.* at 65.

7. *Id.* at 14.

8. *Id.* at 15–17.

9. House Comm. on Gov't Operations, at 18.

10. Select Comm. to Study Governmental Operations with Respect to Intelligence Activities, 94th Cong., Final Report on Intelligence Activities and the Rights of Americans, Book II, I (1976).

11. Katz v. United States, 389 U.S. 347, 353 (1967).

12. United States v. United States Dist. Court, 407 U.S. 297, 321–22 (1972).

13. 124 Cong. Rec. 34,845 (1978).

14. H.R. Rep. No. 95-1283(I), at 50–51 (1978).

15. Intelligence Authorization Act for Fiscal Year 1999, Pub. L. No. 105-272, §§ 601–602, 112 Stat. 2396, 2404 (1998); 50 U.S.C. §§ 1841–1846 (pen and trap).

16. U.S. Dept. of Justice, Civil Rights Div., Disability Rights Section, Title III Highlights, http://www.ada.gov/t3hilght.htm.

17. Self Storage Association, Preamble, 2013 Fact Sheet, http://www.selfstorage.org/ssa/Content/NavigationMenu/AboutSSA/Factsheet/default.htm.

18. 2014 U.S. Car Rental Market: Fleet, Locations and Revenue, http://www.autorentalnews.com/fileviewer/2014.aspx.

CHAPTER ONE

1. Jack Goldsmith, The Terror Presidency 182–183 (2007).

2. James Comey, testimony to Senate Judiciary Committee, *Preserving Prosecutorial Independence: Is the Department of Justice Politicizing the Hiring and Firing of U.S. Attorneys: Part IV*, May 15, 2007.

3. Office of Legal Counsel, Dep't of Justice, Memorandum for the Attorney General, Re: Review of the Legality of the STELLAR WIND program, May 6, 2004, p. 2.

4. USA PATRIOT Act, at § 215, 115 Stat. 272, 287 (emphasis added).

5. 147 Cong. Rec. S10591 (2001) (statement of Sen. Feinstein).

6. *In re* All Matters Submitted to the Foreign Intelligence Surveillance Court, 218 F. Supp. 2d 611 (FISA Ct. Rev. 2002).

7. *In re* Sealed Case, 310 F.3d 717, 735 (FISA Ct. Rev. 2002).

8. 18 USC § 2518(3)(a).

9. 18 USC § 2518(3)(b).

10. Under FISCR's 2002 decision in *In re Sealed Case*, however, this means that the government may use this provision even if the primary end is a criminal investigation.

11. 154 Cong. Rec. H5762 (daily ed. June 20, 2008) (statement of Rep. Harman).

12. 154 Cong. Rec. H5772 (daily ed. June 20, 2008) (statement of Rep. Langevin).

13. 154 Cong. Rec. S6382 (daily ed. July 8, 2008) (statement of Sen. Feingold). In Youngstown Sheet & Tube Co. v. Sawyer, a case that grew out of President Truman's seizure of the steel mills during the Korean War, the Supreme Court rejected the president's claim to inherent authority to take possession of citizens' private property. Youngstown Sheet & Tube Co. v. Sawyer, 343 U.S. 579, 579 (1952) (Jackson, J., concurring). Lawyers and scholars often look to Justice Robert H. Jackson's concurrence in the case, in which he laid out three categories of presidential action, to analyze the province of overlapping authorities. Jackson explained that where the president "acts pursuant to an express or implied authorization of Congress, his authority is at its maximum." *Id.* at 635. At such moments, it includes both the power the president holds "in his own right plus all that Congress can delegate." *Id.* If such an act is deemed unconstitutional, it generally means that the federal government did not have the power in the first place. In the second zone, Jackson suggested, where the president lacks "either a congressional grant or denial of authority, he can only rely upon his own independent powers, but there is a zone of twilight in which he and Congress may have concurrent authority, or in which its distribution is uncertain." *Id.* at 637. This is a harder area for the Court to assess and deeply dependent on the context. The third category Jackson contemplated is "[w]hen the President takes measures incompatible with the expressed or implied will of Congress." Here, "his power is at its lowest ebb." *Id.* The reason the president lacks authority here is because the courts must take account of the extent to which Congress has control over this domain, and essentially subtract it from the authority available to the president. Jackson explained, "Courts can sustain exclusive presidential control in such a case only by disabling the Congress from acting upon the subject." *Id.* at 637–638. Jackson warned, "Presidential claim to a power at once so conclusive and preclusive must be scrutinized with caution, for what is at stake is the equilibrium established by our constitutional system." *Id.* at 638.

14. Letter from DNI James Clapper and AG Eric Holder to John Boehner, Speaker of the House; Harry Reid, Majority Leader, U.S. Senate; Nancy Pelosi, Democratic Leader, U.S. House of Representatives; Mitch McConnell, Republican Leader, U.S. Senate (Feb. 8, 2012).

15. Letter from thirteen Senators to James R. Clapper, Dir. of Nat'l Intelligence, July 26, 2012, http://www.wyden.senate.gov/download/letter-to-dni.

16. 158 Cong. Rec. H5900–5901 (daily ed. Sept. 12, 2012).

17. 158 Cong. Rec. S8461 (daily ed. Dec. 28, 2012).

18. FISA Amendments Act Reauthorization Act of 2012, Pub. L. No. 112-238. 126 Stat. 1631 (2012).

CHAPTER TWO

1. This chapter draws from Laura K. Donohue, *The Dawn of Social Intelligence (SOCINT)*, Drake L. Rev. (2015) (arguing that the emergence of social intelligence, which is grounded in digital data about social relationships, represents a new form of intelligence).

2. Bruce Schneier, Data and Goliath (2015).

3. Alan Rusbridger, *The Snowden Leaks and the Public*, N.Y. Rev. of Books, Nov. 21, 2013.

4. David Cole, "*We Kill People Based on Metadata*," N.Y. Rev. of Books, May 10, 2014.

5. Patrick Mutchler and Jonathan Mayer, *MetaPhone: The Sensitivity of Telephone Metadata*, Web Policy, Mar. 12, 2014, http://webpolicy.org/2014/03/12/metaphone-the-sensitivity-of-telephone-metadata/.

6. Ryan Whitwam, *MIT Researchers Figure out How to Break Tor Anonymity Without Cracking Encryption*, Extreme Tech, Jul. 29, 2015, http://www.extremetech.com/extreme/211169-mit-researchers-figure-out-how-to-break-tor-anonymity-without-cracking-encryption.

7. Associated Press, *U.S. Secretly Created "Cuban Twitter" to Stir Unrest and Undermine Government*, Guardian, Apr. 3, 2014.

8. National Research Council, Protecting Individual Privacy in the Struggle Against Terrorists: A Framework for Program Assessment 2 (2008).

9. REPORT ON THE TELEPHONE RECORDS PROGRAM CONDUCTED UNDER SECTION 215 OF THE USA PATRIOT ACT AND ON THE OPERATIONS OF THE FOREIGN INTELLIGENCE SURVEILLANCE COURT, PRIVACY AND CIVIL LIBERTIES OVERSIGHT BOARD 11 (Jan. 23, 2014).

10. PR/TT, Memorandum Opinion, at 9, http://www.dni.gov/files/documents/1118/CLEANEDPRTT%202.pdf.

11. *Id.* at 3.

12. 50 USC §1842(d)(1)-(2).

13. PR/TT, Memorandum Opinion, at 73, http://www.dni.gov/files/documents/1118/CLEANEDPRTT%202.pdf.

14. *Id.* at 75.

15. *Id.* at 8.

16. 18 USC §3123.

17. ADMINISTRATION WHITE PAPER: BULK COLLECTION OF TELEPHONY METADATA UNDER SECTION 215 OF THE USA PATRIOT ACT 3 (Aug. 9, 2013).

18. REPORT ON THE TELEPHONE RECORDS PROGRAM CONDUCTED UNDER SECTION 215 OF THE USA PATRIOT ACT AND ON THE OPERATIONS OF THE FOREIGN INTELLIGENCE SURVEILLANCE COURT, PRIVACY AND CIVIL LIBERTIES OVERSIGHT BOARD 11 (Jan. 23, 2014).

19. LIBERTY AND SECURITY IN A CHANGING WORLD, PRESIDENT'S REVIEW GROUP ON INTELLIGENCE AND COMMUNICATIONS TECHNOLOGIES 17 (Dec. 12, 2013).

CHAPTER THREE

1. Barton Gellman & Laura Poitras, *U.S., British Intelligence Mining Data from Nine U.S. Internet Companies in Broad Secret Program*, WASH. POST, June 7, 2013; Glen Greenwald & Ewen MacAskill, *NSA Prism Program Taps in to User Data of Apple, Google and Others*, GUARDIAN, June 6, 2013. The Privacy and Civil Liberties Oversight Board later clarified, "Once foreign intelligence acquisition has been authorized under Section 702, the government sends written directives to electronic communication service providers compelling their assistance in the acquisition of communications." PRIVACY AND CIVIL LIBERTIES OVERSIGHT BD., REPORT ON THE SURVEILLANCE PROGRAM

Operated Pursuant to Section 702 of the Foreign Intelligence Surveillance Act 7 (2014).

2. James Ball, *NSA's Prism Surveillance Program: How It Works and What It Can Do*, Guardian, June 8, 2013.

3. 494 U.S. 259, 266 (Rehnquist, C.J.).

4. 494 U.S. 278 (Kennedy, J.) (concurring).

5. Memorandum Opinion, 2011 WL 10945618, at *26.

6. Intelligence Agency Attorney on How "Multi-Communication Transactions" Allowed for Domestic Surveillance, *available at* https://www.eff.org/deeplinks/2013/08/intelligence-agency-attorney-explains-how-multi-communication-transactions-allowed.

7. Att'y Gen. & Dir. of Nat'l intelligence, Semiannual Assessment of Compliance with Procedures & Guidelines Issued Pursuant to Section 702 of the Foreign Intelligence Surveillance Act, Reporting Period: June 1, 2012–Nov. 30, 2012, at A-5 (2013).

8. 154 Cong. Rec. H5763 (daily ed. June 20, 2008) (statement of Rep. Heather Wilson).

9. 154 Cong. Rec. H5771 (daily ed. June 20, 2008) (statement of Rep. Anna Eshoo).

10. 154 Cong. Rec. S6379 (daily ed. July 8, 2008) (statement of Sen. Cardin) (emphasis added).

11. 154 Cong. Rec. H5763 (daily ed. June 20, 2008) (statement of Rep. Sheila Lee).

12. 154 Cong. Rec. H5759 (daily ed. June 20, 2008) (statement of Rep. Robert Scott).

13. 154 Cong. Rec. H5770 (daily ed. June 20, 2008) (statement of Rep. Jackie Speier).

14. 154 Cong. Rec. S6380 (daily ed. July 8, 2008) (statement of Sen. Benjamin Cardin).

15. 154 Cong. Rec. S6396 (daily ed. July 8, 2008) (statement of Sen. Christopher Bond).

16. Rachel King, *Congressman: House Members Not Given Access to NSA Documents*, Wall St. J., Aug. 12, 2013.

17. Gravel v. United States, 408 U.S. 606, 615 (1972).

18. 158 Cong. Rec. S8459 (daily ed. Dec. 28, 2012) (statement of Sen. Ron Wyden).

19. [Redacted], 2011 WL 10945618, at *5–6 (FISA Ct. Oct. 3, 2011).

20. *Id.* at *5 n.14.

21. *Id.* at *6 (footnote omitted) (emphasis added).

22. *Id.* at *6 n.15 (quoting 50 U.S.C. § 1809(a) (2012)).

23. *Id.*

24. [Redacted], 2011 WL 10945618, at *16 (FISA Ct. Oct. 3, 2011).

25. Letter from James R. Clapper, Dir. Nat'l Intelligence, to Sen. Ron Wyden (June 27, 2014), at 2, http://www.wyden.senate.gov/download/?id=184D62F9-4F43-42D2-9841-144BA796C3D3&download=1 [http://perma.cc/N769-3VR7]. *But see* PCLOB Report, *supra* note 2, at 57 (noting that ODNI and NSD consider this number to be overinclusive).

26. [Redacted], 2011 WL 10945618, at *7–8 (FISA Ct. Oct. 3, 2011).

27. Privacy and Civil Liberties Oversight Bd., Report on the Surveillance Program Operated Pursuant to Section 702 of the Foreign Intelligence Surveillance Act 7 (2014).

CHAPTER FOUR

1. This chapter draws from Laura K. Donohue, *The Original Fourth Amendment, 83* Univ. Chicago L. Rev. (2016) (arguing based on historical sources that the use of "unreasonable" in the text of the Fourth Amendment, in the context of the Founding, meant against the "Reason of the Common Law," which amounted to a prohibition on general warrants).

2. Letter from John Adams to William Tudor, Mar. 29, 1817. LbC, Adams papers.

3. Semayne's Case (1604) 77 Eng. Rep. 194, 195 (K.B.).

4. Hugh Ross Williamson, The Gunpowder Plot 196–97 (1951) (noting Coke's removal of two manuscript copies of *A Treatise of Equivocation* and Tresham's suspicious death, possibly due to poison, shortly thereafter).

5. Warrant (Dec. 30, 1621) *in* Sir Edward Coke, 3 Selected Writings of Sir Edward Coke 99 (Steve Sheppard, ed. 2003).

6. Coke to Parliament, Committee of the Whole House, Proceedings and Debates, ff. 100–100v, in CD, III, 149–51 (Apr. 29, 1628) *in* Selected Writings, *supra* note 51, at 58.

7. Edward Coke, The Third Part of the Institutes of the Laws of England 176 (1644).

8. *Id.*

9. *Id.*

10. 2 MATTHEW HALE, HISTORIA PACITORUM CORONAE 150 (1736). *See also id.* at 109–11. Hale similarly considered a general warrant for arrest to be void. 1 MATTHEW HALE, HISTORIA PACITORUM CORONAE 580 (1736).

11. 2 WILLIAM HAWKINS, TREATISE 84 (1716–1721).

12. 5 GEO. III, Debate in the Commons (Jan. 29, 1765).

13. A Speech in Behalf of the Constitution against the Suspending and Dispensing Prerogative, &c. (Dec. 10, 1766).

14. The Case of Seizure of Papers, being an Action of Trespass by John Entick, Clerk, against Nathan Carrington and three other Messengers in ordinary to the King, Court of Common-Pleas, Mich. Term, 6 GEORGE III. (1765) *in* A COMPLETE COLLECTION OF STATE TRIALS AND PROCEEDINGS FOR HIGH TREASON AND OTHER CRIMES AND MISDEMEANORS FROM THE EARLIEST PERIOD TO THE YEAR 1783, 1031, 1066 (Thomas Jones Howell et al., eds., 1816) [hereinafter *Entick v. Carrington*].

15. 3 WILLIAM BLACKSTONE, COMMENTARIES, 288 (1768); 4 WILLIAM BLACKSTONE, COMMENTARIES, at 286–90 (1769).

16. WILLIAM J. CUDDIHY, THE FOURTH AMENDMENT: ORIGINS AND ORIGINAL MEANING 602-1791 379 (2010).

17. Brief of James Otis, Paxton's Case (Mass. Sup. Ct. 24–26 Feb. 1761), *Massachusetts Spy*, Thu., 29 Apr. 1773 (vol. 3, no. 117), p. 1, cols. 1–2.

18. 10 WORKS OF JOHN ADAMS, 247 (1811–1825).

19. 1 JOHN BOUVIER, A LAW DICTIONARY, ADAPTED TO THE CONSTITUTION AND LAWS OF THE UNITED STATES OF AMERICA, AND OF THE SEVERAL STATES OF THE AMERICAN UNION, 708 (1885).

20. A.J. LANGGUTH, PATRIOTS: THE MEN WHO STARTED THE AMERICAN REVOLUTION 22 (1989).

21. Brief of James Otis, *supra* note 15.

22. VIRGINIA DECL. OF RIGHTS, § 10 (June 12, 1776).

23. PENNSYLVANIA DECLARATION OF RIGHTS, §8 (Sept. 28, 1776).

24. 8 WORKS OF JOHN ADAMS, *supra* note 16, 228–71.

25. Oxford English Dictionary, http://www.oed.com/view/Entry/159072?redirectedFrom=reasonable&.

26. MASS. CONST. of 1780, pt. 1, art. XIV.

27. *Id.*

28. In September 1776, Delaware adopted a Declaration of Rights, stating that the absence of an oath would render specific warrants "grievous and oppressive," even as it condemned all general warrants as "illegal." The state constitution went on to refer to the declaration of rights, stating, "no article of the declaration of rights and fundamental rules of this State, agreed to by this convention . . . ought ever to be violated on any pretense whatever." DELAWARE DECLARATION OF RIGHTS, §17 (Sept. 11, 1776). Maryland delegates met between August and November 1776, at which time they drafted and approved the first state constitution. Its Declaration of Rights emphasized limits on search and seizure. The corresponding clauses took several phrases from the Virginia document, further shaping it to fit Blackstone's complete rejection of general warrants. MARYLAND DECL. OF RIGHTS, § 23 (Nov. 3, 1776). North Carolina, which in December 1776 inserted a Declaration of Rights as the first section of its Constitution, eliminated promiscuous search and seizure across the board. It included a section entitled, "General Warrants," in which it made their use for arrest, search, or seizure illegal, on the grounds that the instruments were "dangerous to liberty." NORTH CAROLINA DECLARATION OF RIGHTS, §20 (Dec. 18, 1776).

29. 2 MAX FARRAND, THE RECORDS OF THE FEDERAL CONVENTION OF 1787, 587 (1911).

30. Quoted without citation in PAULINE MAIER, RATIFICATION: THE PEOPLE DEBATE THE CONSTITUTION, 1787–1788 56 (2010).

31. Richard Henry Lee's Proposed Amendments, Sept. 27, 1787, http://csac.history.wisc.edu/confederation_congress.htm.

32. *Debates in the Convention of the Commonwealth of Virginia, on the Adoption of the Federal Constitution, in* 3 DEBATES IN THE SEVERAL STATE CONVENTIONS ON THE ADOPTION OF THE FEDERAL CONSTITUTION, AS RECOMMENDED BY THE GENERAL CONVENTION AT PHILADELPHIA IN 1787 448–49 (Jonathan Elliott ed., 2d ed. Rev. 1891).

33. *Id.* at 588.

34. *Id.* at 657.

35. *Id.* at 658 (emphasis added).

36. *A Son of Liberty*, NEW YORK JOURNAL, Nov. 8, 1787, http://csac.history.wisc.edu/son_of_liberty.pdf (emphasis in the original).

37. *Dated July 26, 1788, signed by George Clinton, President of the Convention, The Ratifications of the Twelve States, in* 1 THE DEBATES IN THE SEVERAL STATE CONVENTIONS ON THE ADOPTION OF THE FEDERAL CONSTITUTION, AS

Recommended by the General Convention at Philadelphia, in 1787 328 (Jonathan Elliot, ed., 2d ed. Rev. 1891) (emphasis added).

38. *Id.*

39. *Fragment of Facts, Disclosing the Conduct of the Maryland Convention, on the Adoption of the Federal Constitution, in* 2 Debates in the Several State Conventions on the Adoption of the Federal Constitution, as Recommended by the General Convention at Philadelphia, in 1787 551–52 (Jonathan Elliott ed., 2d ed. Rev. 1891).

40. Centinel, 13 Independent Gazetteer (Philadelphia), Kaminski & Saladino, No. 1, Oct. 5, 1787, at 328–29.

41. Brutus, # 84.

42. Johnson's Dictionary (1768), defined effects as "Goods; moveables." A general dictionary from 1730 defined it as "the goods of a merchant, tradesman, & c." Dictionarium Britannicum (Nathan Bailey, ed., 1730, reprinted 1969).

43. Boyd v. United States, 116 U.S. 616 (1886).

CHAPTER FIVE

1. This chapter draws from Laura K. Donohue, *The Original Fourth Amendment*, 83 Univ. Chicago L. Rev. (2016) (examining the arguments animating the Founders' prohibition of general warrants).

2. Samuel D. Warren and Louis D. Brandeis, *The Right to Privacy, in* Legal Reasoning 75, 77 (Martin P. Golding ed., 2001).

3. Jonathan Mayer, Patrick Mutchler, and John C. Mitchell, *The Privacy Properties of Telephone Metadata*, Proceedings of the National Academy of Sciences (forthcoming).

4. *Three Degrees of Separation: Breaking Down the NSA's "Hops" Surveillance Method*, Guardian, Oct. 28, 2013.

5. Herbert Broom and George Lewis Denman, Constitutional Law Viewed in Relation to Common Law (1885), p. 608. In light of this argument, it should hardly be surprising that NSA analysts used FISA data to spy on former, current, and potential lovers. In response to an inquiry from Senator Charles Grassley, the NSA Inspector General noted that as of August 2013, there had been a dozen substantiated instances of the misuse

of NSA's surveillance authorities. Incidents ranged from suspected infidelity to use of the database to conduct background checks prior to dating. The practice of monitoring the communications of partners, lovers, and ex and potential girlfriends and boyfriends has earned its own intelligence moniker: LOVEINT.

6. David Burnham, A Law Unto Itself: The IRS and the Abuse of Power (1990).

7. 2 Senate Select Committee on Government Intelligence, Intelligence Activities and the Rights of Americans, S. Rep. No 94–755, at 53–54 (1976).

8. Staff of Joint Comm. on Internal Revenue Taxation, 94th Cong., Rep on Investigation of the Special Services Staff of the Internal Revenue Service 15 (Comm. Print 1975).

9. Ebola Virus Disease, Fact Sheet No. 103, World Health Org, Sept. 2014, http://www.who.int/mediacentre/factsheets/fs103/en/.

10. Proceedings on Error in an Action of False Imprisonment by Dryden Leach, against John Money, James Watson, and Robert Blackmore, three of the King's Messengers, King's-Bench, Eastern Term, 5 George III, and Mich. Term, 6 George III, (1763) *in* A Complete Collection of State Trials and Proceedings, at 1024 [hereinafter *Leach v. Money*].

11. Wilkes v. Wood, Lofft 18, 18, 19 Howell St. Tr. 1153, 1167, 98 Eng. Rep. 489, 498 (C.P. 1763).

12. Grumon v. Raymond, 1 Conn. 40 (1814).

13. Dr. Bonhams's Case, 8 Co.Rep. 107a, 118a, 77 Eng. Rep. 638, 652 (C.P. 1610). The Supreme Court frequently cites back to this case in support of the proposition. *But see* Adrian Vermeule, *Contra Nemo Iudex in Sua Causa: the Limits of Impartiality*, Yale L.J. (2012) (arguing for limits on the principle).

14. Oliver Dickerson, *Writs of Assistance as a Cause of the American Revolution in* The Era of the American Revolution 60–61, 64, 69 (Richard Morris ed., 1939).

15. George G. Wolkins, *Writs of Assistance in England*, in 66 Proceedings of the Massachusetts Historical Society, Third Series 358 (1936–1941).

16. Dianne Feinstein, Statement on Intel Committee's CIA Detention, Interrogation Report, Mar. 11, 2014, http://www.feinstein.senate.gov/public/index.cfm/2014/3/feinstein-statement-on-intelligence-committee-s-cia-detention-interrogation-report.

17. *Id.*

18. Mark Hosenball, *Exclusive: CIA Says Its Inspector General Is Resigning at End of Month*, Reuters, Jan. 5, 2015, http://www.reuters.com/article/2015/01/05/us-usa-cia-inspector-exclusive-idUSKBN0KE1BO20150105.

19. *Minimization Procedures Used by the National Security Agency in Connection with Acquisitions of Foreign Intelligence Information Pursuant to Section 702 of the Foreign Intelligence Surveillance Act of 1978, as amended*, Director of National Intelligence 7 (Jan. 8, 2007), http://www.dni.gov/files/documents/Minimization%20Procedures%20used%20by%20NSA%20in%20Connection%20with%20FISA%20SECT%20702.pdf.

20. *Id.*, at 7–8.

21. Peter Finn, *Guantanamo Dogged by New Controversy After Mishandling of Emails*, Wash. Post, Apr. 11, 2013.

22. Letter from James R. Silkenat, President, American Bar Association, to General Keith B. Alexander, Director, NSA and Rajesh De, General Counsel, NSA, Feb. 20, 2014, http://www.americanbar.org/content/dam/aba/uncategorized/GAO/2014feb20_privilegedinformation_l.authcheckdam.pdf.

23. Letter from Keith B. Alexander, NSA, to James R. Silkenat, ABA, Mar. 10, 2014, http://www.americanbar.org/content/dam/aba/images/abanews/nsa_response_03102014.pdf.

24. 4 William Blackstone, Commentaries on the Laws of England 288 (1769, reprinted facsimile The University of Chicago Press, 1979).

25. 3 Debates in the Several State Conventions on the Adoption of the Federal Constitution, as Recommended by the General Convention at Philadelphia in 1787 588 (Jonathan Elliott ed., 2d ed. Rev. 1891).

CHAPTER SIX

1. Smith v. Maryland, 442 U.S. 735, 744 (1979), quoting United States v. Miller, 425 U.S. 435 (1976).

2. *Id.* at 743–44.

3. United States v. Miller, 425 U.S. 435, 440–41 (1976).

4. Section 215 White Paper, *supra* note 3, at 19.

5. Defendants' Memorandum of Law in Support of Motion to Dismiss the Complaint at 32–33, ACLU v. Clapper, No. 13-cv-03994 (S.D.N.Y. Aug. 26, 2013) (quoting *Smith*, 442 U.S. at 743–44).

6. *Id.* at 33.

7. *In re* Application of the Federal Bureau of Investigation for an Order Requiring the Production of Tangible things from [REDACTED], No. BR 13–109 slip op. at 6. The only other case directly cited in Judge Eagan's Fourth Amendment discussion appears to be a decision of the FISA court itself, with secondary citations. The details of the secret court opinion that she cites as precedent, however, are redacted. *Id.* at 8.

8. *Id.* at 9.

9. 442 U.S. 748.

10. Katz v. United States, 389 U.S. 347, 353 (1967).

11. Olmstead v. United States, 277 U.S. 438, 473 (1928) (Brandeis, J., dissenting).

12. *Id.* at 474–75.

13. United States v. Jones, 132 S. Ct. 945 (2012).

14. *Id.*

15. *Id.* at 947.

16. *Id.* at 953.

17. *Id.* at 963.

18. *Id.*

19. *Id.* at 964.

20. *Id.* at 957 (Sotomayor, J., concurring).

21. *Id.*

22. Kyllo v. United States, 33 U.S. 27, 29, 35 (2001).

23. *Id.* at 48–49.

24. Katz v. United States, 389 U.S. 347, 352 (1967) (emphasis added).

25. Geoffrey R. Stone, *Is the NSA's Bulk Telephony Meta-Data Program Constitutional: Part II*, Huffington Post, Jan. 6, 2014.

26. 468 U.S. 705, 735 (1984) (Stevens, J.).

27. McCulloch v. Maryland, 17 U.S. (4 Wheat.) 316 (1819).

28. Olmstead v. United States, 277 U.S. 438, 472 (1928) (Brandeis, J., dissenting).

29. *Id.* at 473.

30. *Id.* at 474 (footnotes omitted).

31. *Id.* at 476.

CHAPTER SEVEN

1. Scott D. Sagan, *The Problem of Redundancy Problem: Why More Nuclear Security Forces May Produce Less Nuclear Security*, 24(4) RISK ANALYSIS 935 (2004).

2. LAURA K. DONOHUE, THE COST OF COUNTERTERRORISM: POWER, POLITICS, AND LIBERTY 232 (2008); 1 DAVID KRIS & J. DOUGLAS WILSON, NATIONAL SECURITY INVESTIGATIONS AND PROSECUTIONS, 2D ED., 469 (2015); Theodore W. Ruger, *Chief Justice Rehnquist's Appointments to the FISA Court: An Empirical Perspective*, 101 NW. U. L. REV. 239, 245 (2007); Letter from Attorney Gen. William French Smith to Dir., Admin. Office of the U.S. Courts (Apr. 22, 1981).

3. Foreign Intelligence Electronic Surveillance: Hearings on H.R. 5794, H.R. 9745, H.R. 7308, and H.R. 5632 Before the Subcomm. on Legislation of the H. Permanent Select Comm. on Intelligence, 95th Cong. 221 (1978) (statement of the Hon. Laurence H. Silberman) at 217.

4. *In re* Prod. of Tangible Things From [REDACTED], Order Regarding Preliminary Notice of Compliance Incident Dated Jan. 15, 2009, No. BR 08–13, at 4 (FISA Ct. Jan 28, 2009).

5. Memorandum of the United States In Response to the Court's Order Dated Jan. 28, 2009 at 1–2, 11 *In re* Prod. of Tangible Things From [REDACTED], No. BR 08–13 (FISA Ct. Feb. 17, 2009).

6. *In re* Sealed Case, 310 F.3d 717, 719–20 (FISA Ct. Rev. 2002).

7. *In re* Directives [REDACTED] Pursuant to Section 105B of the Foreign Intelligence Surveillance Act, 551 F.3d 1004, 1009–10 (FISA Ct. Rev. 2008).

8. Foreign Intelligence Surveillance Court Rules of Procedure, Nov. 1, 2010, Rule 11, pp. 4–5.

9. *See* Laura K. Donohue, *Technological Leap, Statutory Gap, and Constitutional Abyss: Remote Biometric Identification Comes of Age*, 97 MINN. L. REV. 407–559 (2012).

10. *In re* Directives, 551 F.3d at 1011–12.

11. Clapper v. Amnesty International, 568 U.S. ____ (2013).

12. Yves-Alexandre de Montjoye, Laura Radaelli, Vivek Kumar Singh, Alex "Sandy" Pentland, *Unique in the Shopping Mall: On the Reidentifiability of Credit Card Metadata*, SCIENCE 347, no. 6221, Jan. 29, 2015, 536–539.

Index

. . .